PLATONOV

Also by David Magarshack

★

TURGENEV

★

Translated by David Magarshack

TURGENEV'S LITERARY REMINISCENCES
AND AUTOBIOGRAPHICAL FRAGMENTS

STANISLAVSKY ON THE ART OF THE STAGE

ANTON CHEKHOV

PLATONOV

*A Play
in Four Acts and Five Scenes*

*translated in full
by*
DAVID MAGARSHACK

HILL AND WANG
NEW YORK

© this translation 1964 by David Magarshack
All rights reserved
Library of Congress catalog card number: 64-24827
First edition October 1964

Printed in Great Britain

CONTENTS

INTRODUCTION	*page* 9
ACT I	17
ACT II Sc. 1	65
ACT II Sc. 2	103
ACT III	134
ACT IV	164

(The dialogue between square brackets has been omitted in the BBC broadcast of the play. These omissions may be found useful by prospective producers in making the play more compact and increasing its dramatic impact.)

INTRODUCTION

Platonov, the earliest preserved play of Anton Chekhov, was discovered in manuscript after Chekhov's death and first published in Russia in 1923. The manuscript consists of one hundred and thirty-four closely written pages. As its title page is missing, it was published under the title of *A Play Without a Title in Four Acts*. The four acts of the play are intact, but the text has been corrected many times in black and blue pencil as well as in ink. It is not dated, but an examination of the handwriting shows that it must have been written in the early 'eighties. The play is referred to by Chekhov's younger brother, Michael, in his introduction to the second volume of Chekhov's letters. 'While a student,' Michael writes, 'Chekhov wrote a long play and, hoping to have it performed at the Maly Theatre, took it to the famous actress Yermolova. It was a very unwieldy play, with a railway train, horse thieves, and the lynching of a gipsy.' It is evident from this reference that Michael had only a hazy recollection of the play, for Osip, the only horse thief in it, is not a gipsy. Chekhov himself was so disappointed by the rejection of the play that on his return from the visit to the Maly Theatre, he tore up the clean copy of it. The copy that has been preserved is certainly exceedingly long and 'unwieldy'. His repeated insistence on compactness as one of the most important requirements of a well-written play is most probably the result of his realization that the length of *Platonov* (it runs in the Russian text to over one hundred and sixty-four pages, that is, it is almost as long as his three last plays put together) was its most glaring fault. However, the significant thing about *Platonov* is that it represents Chekhov's first attempt to paint a large canvas of the social forces that were moulding Russian life in the last two decades of the nineteenth century. In spite of its shortcomings, it not only contains a gallery of well-realized portraits taken from the different strata of Russian society, but also shows the clash between the economic forces his characters represent and affords, in a symbolic form, a glimpse of the inevitable outcome of this struggle. It is surely a remarkable fact that at the age of twenty-one, when he was only just becoming known as a writer of humorous trifles, Chekhov should have undertaken a major dramatic work in which he appraised the whole social fabric of his times and passed his judgment upon it. The play, then, is a microcosm of Russia in the 'eighties of the last century. Its characters include the young widow of a general (Anna) and her improvident idealist of a stepson (Sergey Voynitsev), as well as other representatives of the landowning class, and Platonov himself, a former rich landowner who has squandered his patrimony and is now a village teacher, a representative of the army (Colonel Triletsky) and his son, representing the liberal professions.

One of the most remarkable things about *Platonov* is that it contains most of the principal themes of his last great plays. Thus one of the main themes of both *Platonov* and *The Cherry Orchard* is the passing of an old family estate into the hands of rich businessmen.

In *Platonov* the comment of Anna to her stepson Sergey Voynitsev is terse and to the point: 'Well, feudal lord? What are you going to do now? God gave it all to your forefathers and now he has taken it away from you. You've nothing left. You can't help being sorry to have to say goodbye to your country seat, but what can you do, my dear? There is no way of getting it back. It had to be like that.' In *The Cherry Orchard* Lyubov and Varya react violently to the sale of the Ranevsky estate, Lyubov breaking into sobs and Varya flinging the keys on the floor, but Anya is glad the past is done with. 'We shall plant another orchard,' she tells her mother, 'an orchard more splendid than this one.'

The theme of 'a new life', which occurs in *Platonov*, is to be found again in *Ivanov* and, of course, in *The Cherry Orchard*. It is heard again in a more generalized form in *The Three Sisters*.

All through his life Chekhov was obsessed with *Hamlet*. In *Platonov* one of the most revealing dramatic scenes depends on two quotations from Shakespeare's play. The same is true of *The Seagull*, in which the two *Hamlet* quotations at the beginning of Act I help to elucidate the relationship between Konstantin and his mother. In *The Cherry Orchard* Chekhov even repeats the quotation he had used in *Platonov*: 'Ophelia, nymph, in thy orisons be all my sins remembered.' Another characteristic feature of Chekhov's plays is the quite extraordinary complexity of the personal relationships of their characters. But in spite of their most complicated triangular situations, especially in *Platonov* and *The Seagull*, these never obtrude themselves sufficiently to obscure the much more important themes dealing with the meaning of life, man's duty towards his fellow men, work and leisure, the desire in man's heart for a 'new life', for improved social conditions, for justice and fair play. All through his plays—from *Platonov* to *The Cherry Orchard*—Chekhov insists that work is the only remedy against the evils that lead to the disintegration of moral values, evils which he defines in *The Three Sisters* as 'laziness, complacency, and boredom'. Sophia, Sergey Voynitsev's wife, tells Platonov, with whom she was in love five years earlier and with whom she now proposes to run away: 'I'll make you love work. We shall be decent people. We shall live by the sweat of our brows. I shall work, Michael.' When challenged by Platonov to say what she, an educated upper-class woman who has never done a stroke of work in her life, could do at a time when women of a humbler social position can find no work, she replies confidently: 'You'll see. There may be women who are not like me but I am stronger than they. Have faith, Michael.' Faith in the healing powers of work is also one of the main themes of *The Three Sisters*. When the world of illusion, personified by Moscow, the city in which the three sisters spent the happiest days of their lives, crashes about their ears, when Mary's only love affair ends unhappily with Colonel Vershinin's departure with his regiment *and* his wife and children, when Irene's future with a man she respects but does not love ends in disaster with Tusenbach's death in a senseless duel with a jealous bully of an army officer, when Olga's hopes of finding happiness in marriage and children fade away, when the three sisters lose everything they possess and are driven out of their own home—this accumulation of disasters does not break their spirit, for they realize that their only salvation lies in a life devoted to work for their fellow men. 'They're going away from us,' Mary says before the fall of the final curtain, 'and we shall be left alone to start our life anew.' 'We shall live,' Irene says. 'We must live. We must work.' 'Our lives are not finished yet,' Olga declares. 'Let us live!'

From his first to his last play, Chekhov gives the lie to the critics who go on asserting that he is the creator of 'forlorn and ineffectual women'. Sophia in *Platonov*, Nina in *The Seagull*, Sonia in *Uncle Vanya*, the three sisters, Anya in *The Cherry Orchard* are anything but 'forlorn and ineffectual': they are stronger, more active, more conscious of life and the will to live than are the men.

Two more features of Chekhov's plays not lacking in interest are the parts played by the doctors in *Platonov* and *The Three Sisters* and the pistol shots in all his plays except *The Cherry Orchard*. In *Platonov* and *The Three Sisters* the two doctors, Triletsky and Chebutykin, represent, each in his own way, the decay of human values in a civilized society. Neither takes his profession seriously. Their attitude to their patients is lackadaisical and careless. To them the Hippocratic oath is a joke. In the second scene of Act II of *Platonov*, Triletsky flatly refuses to go to visit a patient who has suffered a heart attack. 'What kind of a creature are you?' Platonov adjures him. 'What do you live for? What God are you worshipping, you strange creature?' While Triletsky, however, preserves some semblance of humanity (he is, after all, prevailed upon to go and see the sick shopkeeper), Chebutykin—his *alter ego* in old age—is not a human being at all. 'Perhaps', he mumbles drunkenly in Act III, 'I am not a human being at all, but merely imagine that I have arms and legs and a head. Perhaps I don't exist at all but just imagine that I walk, eat, and sleep. (*He weeps.*) Oh, if only I did not exist!' Chekhov, in fact, has stripped him of all the finer attributes of humanity.

As for the pistol shots, they occur twice on the stage in *Platonov* and in *Ivanov*, forming the dramatic climax of both plays. In *Uncle Vanya* the shooting also takes place on the stage, but the two shots misfire. The shot in *The Seagull* occurs off stage, but, as in *Platonov* and *Ivanov*, forms the climax of the play in the last act. The shot in *The Three Sisters* is not only fired off stage but in the distance. It emphasizes and imparts added poignancy to the reaffirmation of hope of the three sisters.

Finally, the frequent use of pauses in *Platonov* is another link that stamps it as one of Chekhov's seminal plays, whose careful study is of the utmost importance to any serious student of one of the most subtle and technically most accomplished modern dramatists.

Three garbled English translations of the play (less than one-third of the Russian text) have been published since its Russian publication. This is its first unabridged translation into English.

D.M.

THE CHARACTERS

ANNA PETROVNA VOYNITSEV, a general's young widow.
SERGEY PAVLOVICH VOYNITSEV, Anna's stepson.
SOPHIA (SONIA) YEGOROVNA, his wife.
PORFIRY SEMYONOVICH GLAGOLYEV (GLAGOLYEV SR.)
CYRIL PORFIRIVICH GLAGOLYEV (GLAGOLYEV JR.), his son
GERASIM KUZMICH PETRIN
PAVEL PETROVICH SHCHERBUK
} landowners, neighbours of the Voynitsevs.
MARIA YEFIMOVNA GREKOV (MARY), a girl of twenty.
IVAN IVANOVICH TRILETSKY (COL. TRILETSKY), a retired colonel.
NIKOLAI IVANOVICH TRILETSKY (TRILETSKY JR.), his son, a young doctor.
ABRAM ABRAMOVICH VENGEROVICH (VENGEROVICH SR.), a rich Jew.
ISAAC ABRAMOVICH VENGEROVICH (VENGEROVICH JR.), his son, a student.
TIMOFEY GORDEYEVICH BUGROV, a merchant.
MIKHAIL VASILYEVICH PLATONOV, a village teacher.
ALEXANDRA IVANOVNA (SASHA), his wife, daughter of Ivan Triletsky.
OSIP, a thirty-year-old peasant, a horse thief.
MARKO, a court beadle, a little old man.
VASILY
YAKOV } servants of the Voynitsevs.
KATYA
Guests, servants.

The action takes place on the Voynitsev estate in one of the southern provinces.

ACT ONE

A drawing-room in the Voynitsev country house. French windows leading into the garden and two doors into inner rooms. Modern and antique furniture mixed. A grand piano, beside it a music stand and music. A harmonium. Oil paintings in gilt frames.

ANNA *sits at the piano, head bent over the keys.*

TRILETSKY (*enters, walks up to* Anna): Well?
ANNA (*raising her head*): Nothing . . . A bit boring.
TRILETSKY: Let's have a cigarette, my angel. I'm dying for a smoke. Haven't had one since morning. Don't know why.
ANNA (*hands him a packet of cigarettes*): Take all you want. (*They light their cigarettes.*) I'm bored, my dear Nicholas. Awfully bored. Nothing to do. Oh dear! What's more, I don't know what I could do.

[TRILETSKY *takes her hand.*

ANNA: Feeling my pulse? There's nothing wrong with me.
TRILETSKY: No, I'm not feeling your pulse. Just to imprint a kiss. (*He kisses her hand.*) Feels like a soft cushion. What do you put on your hands? They're so white. Lovely hands. Must kiss them again. (*Kisses her hand.*)] Shall we have a game of chess?
ANNA: Oh, very well . . . (*She looks at the clock.*) A quarter past twelve. I expect our visitors must be famished.
TRILETSKY (*sets out the chessboard*): I shouldn't wonder. I'm ravenous myself.
ANNA: I am not asking about you. You're always hungry, though

perpetually munching something. (*They sit down at the chessboard.*) Your move. Moved already? Think first and then move. I'm moving here. You're always hungry.

TRILETSKY: So that's your move, is it? I see... Yes, my dear lady, I'm hungry. When's dinner? Soon?

ANNA: I don't think so. Our cook celebrated our arrival by getting drunk. He's dead to the world. We shall have lunch soon. Seriously, Nicholas, when will you stop being hungry? Eat, eat, eat—it's awful! Such a small man and such a big stomach!

TRILETSKY: Oh, to be sure! Amazing!

[ANNA: You barge into my room and devour half a pie! It wasn't my pie. It's simply disgusting. Your move.

TRILETSKY: How should I know it wasn't yours? All I know is that it would have gone mouldy there if I hadn't eaten it.] Ah, so that's your move, is it? Not bad. And that's mine. You see, if I eat a lot, it means that I'm enjoying good health, and if I am well, you shouldn't grumble. *Mens sana in corpore sano*. Why think? Move, my sweet lady, without thinking. (*Sings.*) Let me tell you, let me tell you...

ANNA: Shut up. You're not letting me concentrate.

TRILETSKY: What a pity a clever woman like you doesn't know anything about gastronomy. Anyone who doesn't know how to eat well is a monster. A moral monster! For—one moment. Don't do that. It's a bad move. Well? Ah, that's different! For the palate, my dear lady, is as important as the ear or the eye. Taste, my sweet child, is one of the five senses which belongs entirely to the science of psychology. Psychology!

ANNA: I do believe you're about to deliver yourself of some witticism. Don't, my dear fellow. I'm sick of your jokes. Besides, the role of jester doesn't suit you. Have you noticed that I never laugh at your jokes? You ought to have noticed it ages ago, I should have thought.

TRILETSKY: Your move, your ladyship. Protect your horse. You don't laugh because you don't appreciate my jokes. Yes, ma'am.

ANNA: What are you gaping at? Your move. What do you think? Will your girl friend come today?

TRILETSKY: She promised to come. Gave me her word.

ANNA: She should have come long ago in that case. It's almost one o'clock. I hope you won't mind my asking you: are you just friends or is it serious?

TRILETSKY: You mean?

ANNA: I mean what I say, Nicholas. [I'm not asking you in order to gossip about it. Tell me as a friend.] What's Mary Grekov to you and you to her? [Tell me frankly without trying to be funny about it. Well? I ask you as a friend, you know.]

TRILETSKY: What's she to me and I to her? I'm afraid I don't know yet.

ANNA: At least...

TRILETSKY: I go to see her, [I chat with her, I pester her,] I put her mama to the expense of regaling me with cups of coffee and —nothing more. Your move. Actually, I see her every second day, sometimes every day even. We go for walks in leafy country lanes. I talk to her about things that interest me, she talks to me about things that interest her, holding me by this button and removing some fluff from my collar. I'm always covered in fluff, you know.

ANNA: And—

TRILETSKY: And nothing. I'm afraid I can't say what I find so attractive about her. [Boredom, love, or something else? I don't know.] After dinner I'm terribly bored with her. I've found out —by the sheerest accident, mind you—that she's bored with me too.

ANNA: So it's love?

TRILETSKY (*shrugging*): Quite possibly. What do you think? Am I in love with her or not?

ANNA: That's charming! Surely it's you who ought to know that.

TRILETSKY: Oh dear, you simply don't understand me! Your move.

ANNA: *I* don't understand you, Nicholas? No woman *could* understand you in a matter of this kind.

(*Pause.*)

TRILETSKY: She's a nice girl.

ANNA: Yes, I like her. Clever little head. Only, mind, don't get her involved in any kind of unpleasantness. Any kind. You usually do, you know. Talk all sorts of nonsense to her, make all sorts of promises, lead her up the garden, [compromise her and drop her.] I'd be terribly sorry for her. What is she doing now?

TRILETSKY: Reads—

ANNA (*laughs*): . . . and studies chemistry?

TRILETSKY: I believe so.

ANNA: A sweet child . . . [Not so fast! You nearly threw a piece off the board.] I like her with that sharp little nose of hers! She might become quite a good scientist.

TRILETSKY: She can't make up her mind what to do, poor child.

ANNA: Please, Nicholas, ask her to come and see me sometimes. [I'll get to know her and—well, I mean, I shan't charge you a fee for it, I'll just—I mean,] we'll find out what she's really like, both of us, and either let her go in peace or take her into consideration . . . Who knows, perhaps . . . (*Pause.*) You see, to me you are just an innocent babe. You have no sense of responsibility at all. That's why I keep interfering in your affairs. Your move. Now my advice is: either have nothing to do with her at all or marry her . . . Mind, I said marry her! No funny business. If you decide to marry the girl, think it over carefully first. Examine her from every possible angle, not just superficially. Think, reflect, discuss—make quite sure there won't be any regrets afterwards. Do you hear?

TRILETSKY: I do indeed. I'm all ears.

ANNA: I know you! You do everything without thinking and you'll marry without thinking. A woman has only to look at you and you're up to all sorts of mischief. You must consult your friends first. (*Bangs the table.*) That's what your head's like. (*Whistles.*) Just the wind whistling through it. Lots of brains, but no sense.

TRILETSKY: Whistles like a peasant. What a woman! (*Pause.*) I don't think she'll come to see you.

ANNA: Why not?

TRILETSKY: Because Platonov is never out of your house. [She can't stand him after all those silly tricks he's played on her.] The man has taken it into his head that she's a fool, and got the idea firmly lodged there and the devil himself can't get it out. For some reason he thinks it's his duty to annoy girls whom he considers to be fools and amuse himself at their expense. Your move. But she isn't a fool, is she? What a rotten judge of people he is!

ANNA: Don't worry, we shan't let him do anything silly. Tell her not to be afraid. But why isn't Platonov here? He should have been here ages ago. (*Looks at the clock.*) It's uncivil of him. We haven't seen each other for six months.

TRILETSKY: I passed his school on my way here. The windows were still shuttered. I expect he must still be asleep. [What a beast of a man! Haven't seen him for a long time myself.]

ANNA: Is he all right?

TRILETSKY: He's always all right. Strong as a horse.

(*Enter* GLAGOLYEV SR. *and* VOYNITSEV)

GLAGOLYEV SR. (*entering*): That's how it is, my dear sir. In this respect we, the setting suns, are much better off and much happier than the rising ones. [As you see, the man hasn't lost and the woman, too, has won.] (*They sit down.*) Let's sit down. I'm tired. We used to love women like true knights. We believed in them and worshipped them, because we regarded them as better human beings. A woman is a better human being, sir!

ANNA: Why are you cheating?

TRILETSKY: Who's cheating?

ANNA: Who put this pawn here?

TRILETSKY: You did!

ANNA: Why, yes, I'm sorry.

TRILETSKY: I should think so too!

GLAGOLYEV SR.: We used to have friends too. When I was young friendship was neither so naïve nor so unnecessary. We used to have all sorts of literary and political circles. And let me tell you, my dear sir, it was a rule with us to go through fire and water for our friends.

VOYNITSEV (*yawns*): Yes, a glorious time!

TRILETSKY: And in these awful times we employ firemen to go through fire for our friends.

ANNA: This is silly, Nicholas. (*Pause*.)

[GLAGOLYEV SR.: Last winter in Moscow I saw a young man weeping at the opera—he was so deeply moved by good music. It's fine, isn't it?

VOYNITSEV: Yes, I suppose it's very fine.

GLAGOLYEV SR.: I think so, too. But why then, tell me, did the young men and women near him look at him and smile? What were they smiling at? He, too, poor fellow, noticing that people saw him crying, began fidgeting in his seat, blushed, smiled stupidly, and then left the theatre. When we were young we were not ashamed of such tears and did not laugh at them.]

TRILETSKY (*to* Anna): I wish this sentimental idiot would die of melancholy. I could wring his neck. Gets on my nerves, he does.

ANNA: Sh-sh . . .

[GLAGOLYEV SR.: We were happier than you. When we were young a man who understood music did not run out of the theatre. He stayed till the end of the opera. I hope I'm not boring you, my dear sir.

VOYNITSEV: Not at all. What's your conclusion then?

GLAGOLYEV SR.: Well . . . And so on and so forth. If we were to draw any conclusion from what I've been saying, it would appear that] in my time people loved and hated, and were, therefore, capable of indignation and contempt.

VOYNITSEV: Excellent, but haven't we got such people now, too?

GLAGOLYEV SR.: I don't think so.

VOYNITSEV gets up and walks towards the window.

GLAGOLYEV SR.: The fact that such people no longer exist explains why we're in such a mess now. (*Pause.*)

VOYNITSEV: Passed unanimously!

ANNA: My goodness, you simply reek of patchuli. I'm going to be sick. (*She laughs.*) Move away a little, please.

TRILETSKY (*moving away*): She's losing and my poor patchuli is at fault. What an extraordinary woman!

[VOYNITSEV: I don't think it's quite fair, sir, to fling about accusations based only on guesswork and on your biassed attitude towards the time when you were young.

GLAGOLYEV SR.: Well, perhaps I am mistaken.

VOYNITSEV: Perhaps? Why, my dear sir, it's not a case of 'perhaps', It's not an accusation that can be dismissed with a laugh.

GLAGOLYEV SR. (*laughs*): But, my dear fellow, there's no need to get hot under the collar. Anyway, this proves—doesn't it—that you're not capable of showing the slightest respect for the views of your opponent.

VOYNITSEV: But, surely, it also proves that I'm capable of getting indignant.

GLAGOLYEV SR.: Well, of course, I'm not saying that everybody is the same. There are exceptions, my dear sir.

VOYNITSEV: Yes, indeed. (*He bows.*) Thank you very much for this little concession. The whole charm of your method lies in these concessions. But what if you happened to come across some inexperienced man, a man who did not know you and who believed that you knew what you were talking about? Why, you would have succeeded in persuading him that we—Nicholas here, my mother, myself and anyone else who is more or less young—are incapable of indignation or contempt.

GLAGOLYEV SR.: But—really you see—er—I never said—]

ANNA: I want to listen to Mr. Glagolyev. Let's finish our game another time.

TRILETSKY: No, no. Play and listen.

ANNA: No, thank you. (*She gets up.*) I've had enough. We'll finish it later.

TRILETSKY: When I'm losing, she seems to be glued to her chair, but the moment I begin to win she wants to listen to Mr. Glagolyev. [(*To* Glagolyev.) And who asked you to speak? You're only interfering with our game. (*To* Anna.) Will you please sit down and continue with our game.] If you don't continue, I shall consider that you've resigned.

ANNA: Consider anything you like! (*She sits down opposite Glagolyev Sr.*)

VENGEROVICH SR. (*enters*): It's hot! [This heat makes me, a Jew, think of Palestine. (*He sits down at the grand piano and runs his fingers over the keys.*) I'm told it's very hot there.]

TRILETSKY (*gets up*): We'll make a note of it. (*He takes out his pocket book.*) We'll make a note of it, my good woman. (*He writes.*) The general's widow, three roubles. Total—ten roubles. Oho! And when, ma'am, shall I have the honour of getting this large sum of money from you?

[GLAGOLYEV SR.: I'm sorry to say, ladies and gentlemen, you have no idea of what it was like in the past. You'd have been singing another tune if you had. You'd have understood ... (*He sighs.*) You'll never understand.

VOYNITSEV: Don't you think, sir, that literature and history have a greater claim on our loyalty? We haven't seen the past, but we feel it. It's here (*slapping the back of his neck*) that we feel it most. It's you, sir, it's you who neither see nor feel the present.]

TRILETSKY: Shall I put it down to your account, your ladyship, or are you going to pay me now?

[ANNA: Do shut up. You're not letting me listen to them.
TRILETSKY: What are you listening to them for? They'll go on talking till the evening.]
ANNA (*to her stepson*): Serge, give this idiot ten roubles.
VOYNITSEV: Ten? (*Takes out his wallet.* [*To* Glagolyev Sr.) Let's change the conversation, sir.
GLAGOLYEV SR.: By all means, if you don't like it.
VOYNITSEV: I like to listen to you, but I refuse to listen to something that is very much like slander.] (*Gives* Triletsky *ten roubles.*)
TRILETSKY: Thanks. (*Slaps* Vengerovich *on the shoulder.*) That's the way to get on in this world. Put a defenceless woman at a chessboard and clean her out of ten roubles without the slightest twinge of conscience.
VENGEROVICH SR.: Congratulations, doctor. [You're a real Jerusalem nobleman.]
ANNA: Stop it, Triletsky. (*To* Glagolyev Sr.) So in your opinion a woman is a much better human being?
GLAGOLYEV SR.: Certainly.
ANNA: Well, you seem to be a great feminist, my dear Mr. Glagolyev.
GLAGOLYEV SR.: Yes, I'm fond of women. I adore them. I see in them everything I like: heart and . . .
ANNA: You adore them, but are they worthy of your adoration?
GLAGOLYEV SR.: Yes, they are.
ANNA: Are you sure? Quite sure, or are you just imagining it?

> TRILETSKY *picks up the violin and begins scraping it with the bow.*

GLAGOLYEV SR.: I'm quite sure. I have only to know you to be sure of it.
ANNA: Seriously? Well, you're certainly original.
VOYNITSEV: He's a romantic.
GLAGOLYEV SR.: Perhaps. I don't mind. Romanticism is not such a

bad thing. You've thrown out romanticism. I suppose you can't be blamed for that, but I'm afraid you've thrown out something else with it.

ANNA: Please, don't let's have an argument about it. [I can't argue. Whether we've thrown it out or not, we've certainly become more intelligent. We have, haven't we? And that's the main thing.] (*Laughs.*) So long as we have intelligent people and they are getting more and more intelligent, the rest will look after itself. Stop that awful noise, Nicholas! Put the violin away.

TRILETSKY (*hangs up the violin*): A lovely instrument!

GLAGOLYEV SR.: Platonov once put it very well. We've grown more intelligent about women, he said, and to become more intelligent about women means to drag women as well as ourselves through the mire.

TRILETSKY (*bursts into loud laughter*): I expect he must have had a cup too many on his birthday when he said that.]

ANNA: Did he say that? (*She laughs.*) Yes, he likes to say something horrid like that sometimes. But he said it merely to be original. Talking of Platonov, what kind of person do you think he is? [Is he a hero or not a hero?]

GLAGOLYEV SR.: Well, how shall I put it? In my opinion Platonov is an admirable representative of our modern uncertainty. He is the hero of the best, though, unfortunately, still unwritten, modern novel. (*He laughs.*) By uncertainty I mean the present condition of our society: the Russian novelist feels this uncertainty. He finds himself in a quandary, he is at a loss, doesn't know what to concentrate on. He doesn't understand—you see, it's so difficult to understand—these people. (*He points at* Voynitsev.) His novels are abominably bad, everything in them is forced and cheap, and, well, no wonder! Everything is so uncertain, so unintelligible ... Everything is so terribly confused. Everything is in such a hopeless muddle. And our highly intelligent Platonov, in my opinion, expresses this uncertainty admirably. How is he, by the way?

ANNA: I'm told he's fine. (*Pause.*) A nice fellow.

GLAGOLYEV SR.: Yes. One can't help respecting him. [I went to see him several times last winter and I shall never forget the few hours I was fortunate enough to spend with him.]

ANNA (*looks at the clock*): It's time he was here. Sergey, did you send for him?

VOYNITSEV: Twice.

ANNA: You're talking a lot of nonsense, gentlemen. Triletsky, run and send Yakov for him.

TRILETSKY (*stretching himself*): Shall I also tell them to lay the table?

ANNA: I'll tell them myself.

TRILETSKY (*walks towards the door and bumps into Bugrov*): Puffing like a railway engine, the dear old grocery man! (*Slaps Bugrov on the stomach and goes out.*)

BUGROV (*entering*): Phew! Devilishly hot! Before the rain, I suppose.

VOYNITSEV: Have you come from the garden?

BUGROV: Yes, sir.

VOYNITSEV: Is Sophia there?

BUGROV: Who's Sophia?

VOYNITSEV: My wife.

VENGEROVICH SR.: One moment! (*He goes out into the garden.*)

Enter PLATONOV *and* SASHA *in Russian national dress.*

PLATONOV (*in the doorway, to* Sasha): After you, young woman. (*He comes in after* Sasha.) Here we are at last! Say how-d'you-do, Sasha. How do you do, your ladyship? (*He goes up to* Anna, *kisses one hand, then the other.*)

ANNA: Cruel, uncivil brute! How could you make us wait so long, you beast! Don't you know how impatient I am? My dear Sasha . . . (*She exchanges kisses with* Sasha.)

PLATONOV: Well, we've got away from home at last, thank God. For six months we haven't seen a parquet floor, or armchairs, or high ceilings, or even people. Hibernated in our lair all winter like bears and only today have we crawled out into the world. My dear Sergey! (*He exchanges kisses with* Voynitsev.)

VOYNITSEV: You've grown taller and put on weight and goodness only knows what else. Heavens, Sasha, you've put on weight, too. (*He shakes hands with* Sasha.) Are you well? Grown plumper and prettier!

PLATONOV (*shakes hands with* Glagolyev Sr.): Very pleased to meet you, sir.

ANNA: How are you, Sasha? How are things with you? Please, sit down—everybody. Tell us all about it. Let's sit down.

[PLATONOV (*bursts out laughing*): My dear Sergey, is it really you? Good Lord, what's happened to your long hair, your lovely shirt and your charming tenor voice? Come on, say something.

VOYNITSEV: I am a damn fool. (*Laughs.*)

PLATONOV: A bass, a real bass. Well, I'm hanged! Let's sit down. (*He sits down.*) Sit down, ladies and gentlemen. Whew! It's terribly hot. Well, Sasha, do you smell something?

They all sit down.

SASHA: I do. (*Laughter.*)

PLATONOV: Smells of human flesh. Wonderful smell!] I feel as though we haven't seen each other for a hundred years. The winter was so hellishly long. There's my armchair. Do you recognize it, Sasha? Six months ago I used to spend days and nights in it searching for the cause of all causes with her ladyship and losing your shining ten-copeck pieces. It's hot! . . .

ANNA: I was worn out with waiting for you. Lost patience. Are you all right?

PLATONOV: Very well, indeed. I hope your ladyship won't mind my telling you that you've grown plumper and just a little bit more beautiful. [It's so hot and close today. I'm already beginning to miss the cold weather.]

ANNA: How horribly fat they've both grown! [What a fortunate couple!] How is life, Platonov?
PLATONOV: Rotten as usual. Slept through the whole winter and never saw the sky for six months. Ate, drank, slept. [Read Mayne Reid to my wife.] Rotten!
SASHA: Oh, it wasn't so bad. A little boring, of course.
PLATONOV: Not a little, my darling, but very boring. Missed you terribly. You're a sight for sore eyes. [To see you, my dear Anna, after such a long wearisome time of not seeing any people or only horrible people—why, it's unbelievable luxury!]
ANNA: Here, have a cigarette for that! (*She gives him a cigarette.*)
PLATONOV: Thanks. (*They light their cigarettes.*)
[SASHA: When did you arrive? Yesterday?
ANNA: Yes, at ten o'clock.
PLATONOV: I saw lights in your house at eleven, but I was afraid to call. I expect you must have been tired.
ANNA: What a pity you didn't call. We sat up talking till two.]

SASHA *whispers something in* PLATONOV's *ear*.

PLATONOV: Good Lord! (*He slaps his forehead.*) What a memory! Why didn't you tell me before? Sergey!
VOYNITSEV: Yes?
PLATONOV: And not a word from him! Gets married and keeps quiet about it. (*Getting up.*) I forgot, and they don't say a thing.
SASHA: I forgot, too, while he was talking. (*To* Voynitsev.) Congratulations! I wish you everything—everything!
PLATONOV: Congratulations! You've performed a miracle, my dear chap. I never expected you to take such an important and courageous step. [So soon and so quick. Who could have expected such a heresy of you?]
VOYNITSEV: Not bad, am I? [Both soon and quick! (*He bursts out laughing.*) I did not expect such a heresy of myself, either. The whole thing, my dear chap, was all over in a twinkling.] Fell in love and got married!

PLATONOV: [Hardly a winter passed without your falling in love, but this winter you also got married, providing yourself with 'a censorship', as our priest says. For a wife is the most terrible and the most fault-finding censorship. If she's a fool, you're done for. Have you] found a job?

VOYNITSEV: I've been offered a job in a prep-school, but I haven't made up my mind whether to take it or not. I don't relish teaching in a prep school. The salary is rather small and, besides—

[PLATONOV: Are you going to take it?

VOYNITSEV: At the moment I'm not sure of anything. Probably not.]

PLATONOV: I see, so we're just going to do nothing as before. It's three years since you got your degree, isn't it?

VOYNITSEV: Yes.

PLATONOV: I see. (*He sighs.*) There's no one to give you a good hiding! I'll have to tell your wife about it. Waste three whole years!

ANNA: It's too hot now for discussing serious matters. I can't help yawning. Why have you been so long calling, Sasha?

SASHA: [I'm afraid we were rather busy. Michael was mending the bird-cage and I went to church. The cage was broken and we couldn't leave our nightingale like that.

GLAGOLYEV SR.: But why go to church today? It isn't a feast day, is it?

SASHA: No,] I went to see Father Konstantin to order a requiem mass. Today's the name day of Michael's late father and, somehow, I felt it wouldn't have been right not to go to church. So I had the requiem mass said for him. (*Pause.*)

GLAGOLYEV SR.: How long is it since your father died, Platonov?

PLATONOV: Some three or four years.

SASHA: Three years and eight months.

GLAGOLYEV SR.: Is it really? Good Lord, how time flies! Three years and eight months! It seems only yesterday that we met for the last time. (*He sighs.*) The last time I met him was at

Ivanovka. We were serving on the same jury. Something happened then that was so typical of him. In the dock, I remember, was a poor land surveyor. A habitual drunkard. He was accused of bribery and corruption and (*he laughs*) we found him not guilty. Your father, Platonov, insisted on his acquittal. He went on arguing for three hours and got terribly excited. 'I shan't find him guilty,' he kept shouting, 'till you declare on oath that you never take bribes yourselves!' Illogical, but—you couldn't do anything with him. Exhausted us, he did. The late General Voynitsev, your late husband, Madam, was on the jury with us. He, too, wasn't a very easy-going man.
ANNA: He would never have acquitted him.
GLAGOLYEV SR.: Well, he insisted on a verdict of guilty. I remember them both very well—red in the face, fierce-looking, boiling over with rage . . . The peasants on the jury were all on the side of the General, and we—the noblemen—were on the side of Platonov. We won, of course. (*He laughs.*) Your father challenged the general to a duel, called him, I'm sorry to say, a scoundrel. It was great fun! We got them drunk and they made it up. There's nothing easier than to get two Russians to make it up. Your father was a kind man. He had a kind heart.
PLATONOV: Not kind, sentimental.
GLAGOLYEV SR.: A great man in his way. I respected him. I was on excellent terms with him.
PLATONOV: Well, I'm afraid I can't say that. I quarrelled with him when I hadn't a hair on my chin and during the last three years of his life we were real enemies. I did not respect him. He considered me a shallow, superficial person—and, I suppose, we were both right. I never liked him, and I still don't like him because he died peacefully. He died as honest men die. To be a blackguard and at the same time to refuse to recognize it—that is the terrible characteristic of the Russian scoundrel.
GLAGOLYEV SR.: *De mortuis aut bene, aut nihil*, my dear fellow.
PLATONOV: No, sir. That is a Latin heresy. In my view: *de omnibus*

aut nihil, aut veritas. It's more educational at any rate. I take it that dead men do not require any concessions.

COL. TRILETSKY *enters.*

COL. TRILETSKY: Well, well, well, my son-in-law and my daughter! Stars from the constellation Triletsky! How are you, my dears? A salute to you from a Krup gun! Good God, it's hot! Michael, my dear fellow!

PLATONOV (*gets up*): How d'you do, Colonel. (*He embraces him.*) Are you well?

COL. TRILETSKY: I'm always well. The good Lord puts up with me and doesn't punish me. Sasha, my darling! (*Kisses* Sasha *on the head.*) Haven't clapped eyes on you for a long time. Are you all right, Sasha?

SASHA: Yes, father. And you?

COL. TRILETSKY (*sits down beside* Sasha): I'm always well. Never had a day's illness in my life. Haven't seen you for a long time. Every day I intend to call on you to see my grandson and to find fault with the ways of the world with my dear son-in-law, but, damn it, something always happens to prevent me. Am busy, my angels. Busy. I was just about to go to see you the day before yesterday to show you, Michael, my double-barrel shotgun, but the district police officer stopped me and I had to join him in a game of preference. Lovely shotgun. English. Hits the target dead on at a hundred and seventy feet. I hope my grandson's all right.

SASHA: Yes, father. He sends his regards.

COL. TRILETSKY: Good Lord, can he do that?

COYNITSEV: You must take it metaphorically.

VOL. TRILETSKY: Oh! Very well, very well. Metaphorically. Tell him, Sasha, to grow up quickly. I'll take him shooting. Got a little shotgun specially for him. Damn me, if I won't make a sportsman of him. Want to leave my hunting trophies to him when I'm gone.

ANNA: The colonel's such a darling. I shall go shooting quail with him on St. Peter's Day.

COL. TRILETSKY: Ho-ho! Quail? Why, my dear lady, we shall organize a campaign against snipe. A Polar expedition to the Devil's Dyke.

ANNA: We'll try out your new double-barrel gun, Colonel!

COL. TRILETSKY: So we shall, so we shall, divine Diana! (*He kisses her hand.*) Remember last year, dear lady? Ha-ha! I like high-spirited women like you, damme! Can't stand timid creatures. Women's emancipation! Why, bless my soul, here you have the best example before you! Smell her lovely shoulder and you get a whiff of gunpowder. She reeks of Hannibals and Hamilcars! A field-marshal, a regular field-marshal! Give her a pair of epaulettes and she'll conquer the world. We'll go shooting, ma'am. And take Sasha with us! Take 'em all with us. We'll show 'em what a soldier's blood's like, divine Diana, Alexandra of Macedon!

PLATONOV: Knocked back a few already, have you, Colonel?

COL. TRILETSKY: Certainly, my boy! Without a shadow of a doubt!

PLATONOV: So that's why you're clacking away so merrily.

COL. TRILETSKY: My dear boy, I came here at eight this morning. Everyone was still asleep. Well, so I walked in here and kicked up a din. Then she came in. Laughing she was. Well, so we opened a bottle of Madeira. Diana here had three glasses and I had the rest of the bottle.

ANNA: Trust you to tell them about it!

TRILETSKY runs in.

TRILETSKY: Greetings to my relations!

PLATONOV: Ah-h! Her ladyship's no-good physician-in-ordinary. *Argentum nitricum—aquae destillate.* Very glad to see you, my dear chap! A picture of health. Shines, sparkles, exudes sweet perfume!

TRILETSKY (*kisses* Sasha's *head*): Quite fantastic the way the devils have blown out your Michael. A bull, a veritable bull!

SASHA: Gracious, you reek of scent! How are you?

TRILETSKY: In the pink! A good thing you came. (*He sits down.*) How are things, Michael?

PLATONOV: Which things?

TRILETSKY: Yours, of course.

PLATONOV: Mine? I'm sure I don't know. It's a long story. Not a very interesting one, either. [Where did you get that beautiful haircut? First class! How much did you pay for it? A rouble?

TRILETSKY: My hair's not cut by hairdressers. I've got ladies who do my hair and it's not for haircuts that I pay them roubles. (*He eats fruit lozenges.*) You see, my dear fellow, I—

PLATONOV: Going to make a joke? Don't do it, there's a good chap! Spare me your jokes, please.]

PETRIN *enters with a newspaper and sits down.* VENGEROVICH SR. *enters and sits down in a corner of the room.*

[TRILETSKY (*to his father*): Weep, father!

COL. TRILETSKY: Why should I weep?

TRILETSKY: Why? For joy. Look at me. I am your son. (*He points at* Sasha.) This is your daughter! (*He points at* Platonov.) This young man is your son-in-law! Think what your daughter alone is worth. A pearl, a veritable pearl, Father! Only you could have begotten such a ravishing daughter! And your son-in-law?

COL. TRILETSKY: Why then should I weep, my friend? I don't want to weep.

TRILETSKY: And your son-in-law? Why, you wouldn't find another such son-in-law if you looked for him all over the universe. Honest, honourable, generous, just! And your grandson? What a boy, what a little devil of a boy! Waves his little hands about, stretches out his arms and squeals, Grandpa, grandpa! Where's grandpa! Give me my Grandpa, the rascal! I want to pull him by his huge moustaches.

COL. TRILETSKY (*pulls out a handkerchief*): I can't see what there is to cry about. Well, thank God. (*He cries.*) There's nothing to cry about.

TRILETSKY: Are you crying, Colonel?

COL. TRILETSKY: No. Why should I be crying? Well, thank God.

PLATONOV: Stop it, Nicholas.]

TRILETSKY (*gets up and sits down beside* Bugrov): It's like an oven here today, sir.

BUGROV: Aye. That is so. As hot as on the top shelf of a bath-house. About thirty, I reckon.

TRILETSKY: What could it mean? Why do you think it's so hot?

BUGROV: You ought to know better than I, doctor.

TRILETSKY: I don't know. I only studied medicine.

BUGROV: Well, sir, in my opinion, it's so hot because we should have died laughing, you and I, sir, if it had been cold in the month of June.

Laughter.

TRILETSKY: I see... Now I understand. [What's more important for the grass, sir? Temperature or rainfall?

BUGROV: Everything's all right, doctor. For corn, though, rain is more desirable. What's the use of a heat wave if there's no rain? Without rain, it isn't worth a brass farthing.

TRILETSKY: I see.] Very true. Very true. Wisdom itself speaks through your lips, sir. [And what is your opinion, Mr. Grocery-man, regarding everything else?

BUGROV (*laughs*): I haven't any.

TRILETSKY: Q.E.D.] You're a most intelligent person, sir. Well, and what would you say about an astronomic conjuring trick to make our hostess give us something to eat? Eh?

ANNA: Wait, Triletsky. We're all waiting, so you can wait too.

TRILETSKY: She doesn't know our appetites. [She doesn't know how much you and I, especially you, my dear sir, want a drink.

And] there's plenty of lovely food and drink there, sir. [To begin with . . . to begin with . . . (*He whispers in* Bugrov's *ear*.) Not bad, eh? But that's just the vodka. *Crematum simplex*. There's everything there: for consumption off and on the premises . . . Then there's] caviar, sturgeon, salmon, sardines . . . six or seven layered pie . . . as big as that. [Stuffed with all sorts of wonders of the flora and fauna of the Old and New Testaments . . .] If only we could have it now! [Are you very hungry sir! Frankly . . .]

SASHA (*to* Triletsky): You don't want to eat so much as to start a riot. You don't like people to sit quietly.

[TRILETSKY: I don't like people to be starved, fatty!

PLATONOV: Is that an example of your sense of humour, Nicholas? Why isn't anyone laughing?]

ANNA: Oh, I'm sick and tired of him! His insolence is positively shocking. It's awful. Can't you wait, you horrid man? All right, I'll go and get you something to eat. (*She goes out*.)

TRILETSKY: About time, too.

PLATONOV: Well, I wouldn't mind having a bite myself . . . What's the time? I'm hungry too.

VOYNITSEV: I wonder where my wife is. You haven't seen her yet, have you, Platonov? I must introduce you to her. (*He gets up*.) [I'd better go and look for her. She likes the garden so much she can't tear herself away from it.]

PLATONOV: As a matter of fact, I'd rather you didn't introduce me to your wife. I'd like to see whether she recognizes me. I used to know her a little a long time ago—and . . .

VOYNITSEV: You knew her? Sophy?

PLATONOV: Yes, once upon a time. I was a student at the time. Don't introduce her to me, please, and don't say anything to her. Not a word.

VOYNITSEV: Very well. This man seems to know everyone! [Where does he find time to know them all I'd like to know.] (*He goes out into the garden*.)

TRILETSKY: What a marvellous article I've just published in the *Russian Courrier*, gentlemen! Have you read it? Have *you* read it, Mr. Vengerovich?

VENGEROVICH SR.: I have.

TRILETSKY: Don't you agree it's a splendid article? I wrote you up as a real man-eating tiger, didn't I? Enough to make the whole of Europe gasp with horror.

PETRIN (*roars with laughter*): So that's who it is? So that's who this V. is! But who, pray, is B.?

BUGROV (*laughs*): That's me. (*He mops his brow.*) Who cares?

VENGEROVICH SR.: Not bad, not bad at all. If I knew how to write, I'd certainly write for the papers. To begin with, you get paid for it, and, secondly, we seem for some reason inclined to assume that people who write are highly intelligent. Only I'm afraid, doctor, you didn't write that article at all. Mr. Glagolyev wrote it.

GLAGOLYEV SR.: How do you know that?

VENGEROVICH SR.: I know.

GLAGOLYEV SR.: That's funny . . . It's true I wrote it, but how the devil did you find out?

VENGEROVICH SR.: Oh, one can find out everything if one wants to badly enough. You sent it off by registered post and—well—the clerk at the office has a good memory. That's all. There's nothing mysterious about it. My Jewish cunning has nothing to do with it . . . (*He laughs.*) Don't be afraid. I'm not going to do anything about it.

GLAGOLYEV SR.: I'm not afraid, but it's still a bit peculiar. (*Enter Mary Grekov.*)

TRILETSKY (*jumps up*): Mary! This is nice! A real surprise!

MARY (*gives him her hand*): How are you, Triletsky? (*She nods to the rest in the room.*) Good afternoon, gentlemen. (Triletsky *helps her off with her cloak.*)

TRILETSKY: Let me take your cloak. How are you? (*He kisses her hand.*)

MARY: Just as usual . . . (*She is overcome with confusion and sits down on the first available chair.*) Is Mrs. Voynitsev at home?

TRILETSKY: She is. (*He sits down beside her.*)

GLAGOLYEV SR.: How do you do, Miss Grekov?

COL. TRILETSKY: Is this the Grekov girl? Bless my soul, I hardly recognized her. (*He goes up to* Mary *and kisses her hand.*) Very pleased to see you, my dear.

MARY: How do you do, Colonel? (*She coughs.*) It's awfully hot! Please don't kiss my hand. It makes me feel embarrassed. I don't like it.

PLATONOV (*walks up to* Mary): How do you do? (*He wants to kiss her hand.*) Do give me your hand!

MARY (*snatching her hand away*): Thank you, no.

PLATONOV: Why not? You don't object to me, do you?

MARY: No. But you . . . you don't really want to, do you?

PLATONOV: How do you know I don't want to?

MARY: You wouldn't have wanted to kiss my hand if I hadn't said that I didn't like it. You seem to like doing what I dislike.

PLATONOV: You *do* jump to conclusions!

TRILETSKY (*to* Platonov): Go away!

PLATONOV: One moment . . . How is your bedbug ether getting on, my dear Miss Grekov?

MARY: What ether?

PLATONOV: I heard you were extracting ether from bedbugs. To benefit science, I suppose. An excellent thing.

MARY: You're always joking.

TRILETSKY: Yes, he's always joking. So here you are, Mary. How's your mother?

PLATONOV: What lovely rosy cheeks you've got. You're not too hot, are you?

MARY (*getting up*): Why are you saying all this to me?

PLATONOV: I want to talk to you. I haven't talked to you for ages. Why are you so angry? When will you stop being angry with me?

MARY: I've noticed that you're not your natural self when you see me. I'm sure I don't know what I do to provoke you ... I'm trying to avoid you as much as possible. Had not Nicholas given me his word of honour that you wouldn't be here, I shouldn't have come. (*To* Triletsky.) You ought to be ashamed to tell lies!

PLATONOV: You ought to be ashamed to tell lies, Nicholas! (*To* Mary.) I believe you're about to cry. Do cry. Tears are a great help sometimes ...

    MARY *goes quickly to the door where she meets* ANNA.

TRILETSKY (*to* Platonov): It's silly—damn silly! Understand? Damn silly! Next time you'll have me to answer to.

PLATONOV: What have you to do with it?

TRILETSKY: Silly! You don't know what you're doing.

GLAGOLYEV SR.: It was cruel, sir.

ANNA: My dear Mary, I'm so glad ... (*She presses* Mary's *hand.*) Very glad. You are such a rare visitor. But you've come at last and I love you for it. Let's sit down. (*They sit down.*) Very glad! I'm grateful to Nicholas. He went to great trouble to persuade you to come from your village.

TRILETSKY (*to* Platonov): Suppose I love her, what then?

PLATONOV: Well, love her. [Do me a favour.]

TRILETSKY: You don't know what you're saying!

ANNA: How are you, my dear?

MARY: I'm all right, thank you.

ANNA: You look tired. (*She looks closely at her.*) It must be an awful bore driving for twenty miles when you're not used to it.

MARY: No ... (*She puts handkerchief to her eyes and cries.*) No ...

ANNA: What's the matter, Mary? (*Pause.*)

MARY: No ...

    TRILETSKY *paces up and down the stage.*

GLAGOLYEV SR. (*to* Platonov): You ought to apologize, sir.

PLATONOV: Whatever for?

GLAGOLYEV SR.: Don't you know? You were cruel.

SASHA (*goes up to* Platonov): Apologize, or I'll leave. Go and say you're sorry.

ANNA: I sometimes cry myself after a long journey. One's nerves get so frayed.

GLAGOLYEV SR.: Look here, I insist that you apologize! It's ungracious. I didn't expect it of you.

SASHA: Apologize, I tell you. You brute!

ANNA: Oh, I understand now. (*She looks at* Platonov.) He's done it! I'm sorry, Mary. I forgot to have a talk with this—this—It's my fault.

PLATONOV (*going up to* Mary): Miss Grekov!

MARY (*raises her head*): What do you want?

PLATONOV: I am sorry. I apologize to you in public. I'm consumed with shame! Give me your hand. I swear I'm sincere. (*He takes her hand.*) Let's make it up. No more whimpering, please. Peace? (*He kisses her hand.*)

MARY: Peace. (*She covers her face with a handkerchief and runs out, followed briskly by* Triletsky.)

ANNA: I never thought you'd do a thing like that! You!

GLAGOLYEV SR.: Prudence, my dear fellow. Prudence, for God's sake!

PLATONOV: Enough. (*He sits down on the sofa.*) Don't let's talk about her. It was stupid of me to speak to her and it's no use wasting a lot of words on stupidity.

ANNA: Triletsky shouldn't have gone after her. Not every woman likes to be seen crying.

GLAGOLYEV SR.: I respect this sensitiveness in women. After all, I don't suppose you said anything particular to her, but—a hint, a word . . .

ANNA: You shouldn't have done it, Michael. It's not nice.

PLATONOV: But I have apologized, haven't I?

Enter VOYNITSEV, SOPHIA, [*and* VENGEROVICH JR.].

VOYNITSEV (*rushing in*): She's coming, she's coming! (*He sings.*) She's coming!

[VENGEROVICH JR. *stops at the door with arms folded on his chest.*]

ANNA: At last Sophia has had enough of this horrible heat. Come in, come in!

PLATONOV (*aside*): Sonia! Heavens, how she's changed!

SOPHIA: I was so interested talking to Mr. Vengerovich that I forgot all about the heat. (*She sits down on the sofa, some distance away from* Platonov.) I'm simply thrilled with your garden, Sergey.

GLAGOLYEV SR. (*sits down beside* Sophia): Sergey!

VOYNITSEV: Yes, sir?

GLAGOLYEV SR.: Your wife, my dear fellow, has promised me that you will all call on me next Thursday.

PLATONOV (*aside*): She looked at me.

VOYNITSEV: We shall certainly keep her promise. We shall come to see you, all of us.

TRILETSKY (*comes in*): Oh, women, women! said Shakespeare, and he was wrong. He should have said: Oh you, women!

ANNA: Where's Mary?

TRILETSKY: I took her into the garden. I hope she'll get over her upset there.

GLAGOLYEV SR.: You've never been to my house, Sophia, have you? I hope you'll like it. My garden is better than yours. A deep river, good horses . . . (*Pause.*)

ANNA: Silence . . . A fool's been born. (*Laughter.*)

SOPHIA (*softly, to* Glagolyev Sr., *motioning to* Platonov *with her head.*): Who's that? The one sitting on the sofa next to me.

GLAGOLYEV SR. (*laughs*): It's our schoolmaster. [Don't know his surname.]

[BUGROV (*to* Triletsky): Tell me, please, doctor. Can you cure all illnesses or only some?

TRILETSKY: All.
BUGROV: Anthrax, too?
TRILETSKY: Yes. Anthrax, too.
BUGROV: And if a mad dog bit me, could you cure that, too?
TRILETSKY: Why, has a mad dog bitten you? (*He moves away from him.*)
BUGROV (*taken aback*): Good Lord, no. What are you saying? (*Laughter.*)]
ANNA: How do we get to your place, Mr. Glagolyev? [Through Yusnovka?
GLAGOLYEV SR.: No. You'll make a detour if you drive through Yusnovka.] You have to drive straight to Platonovka itself. I live quite near, just about a mile and a half from Platonovka.
SOPHIA: I know of Platonovka. Does it still exist?
GLAGOLYEV SR.: Why, yes.
SOPHIA: I used to know its owner, Platonov. Sergey, have you any idea where Platonov is now?
PLATONOV (*aside*): Why doesn't she ask me where he is?
VOYNITSEV: I believe I know. You don't remember his name do you? (*He laughs.*)
PLATONOV: I used to know him too. I believe his name is Michael. (*Laughter.*)
SOPHIA: Yes, yes. His name is Michael. I knew him when he was still a student, almost a boy. You're laughing. I'm afraid I don't see anything to laugh at.
ANNA (*bursts out laughing and points at* Platonov): For goodness' sake recognize him or he'll burst with suspense.

PLATONOV *gets up.*

SOPHIA (*gets up and looks at* Platonov): Yes. It's him. Why don't you say anything? Is it—you?
PLATONOV: Don't you recognize me? No wonder. Four and a half years, almost five years, have passed and no rats can ravage a man's face so much as my last five years have done.

SOPHIA (*gives him her hand*): I'm only just beginning to recognize you. How you have changed!
VOYNITSEV (*takes Sasha to Sophia*): And this is his wife Alexandra, the sister of one of our wittiest men, Nicholas Triletsky.
SOPHIA (*shakes hands with Sasha*): Very pleased to meet you. (*She sits down.*) So you're married, too. Long ago? Still, five years is a long time.
ANNA: What a man! Never goes anywhere but knows everyone. He's one of our closest friends, Sophy.
PLATONOV: This wonderful introduction gives me the right to ask you how you are. What have you been doing with yourself, Sophia?
SOPHIA: Oh, nothing in particular. I've not been feeling too well lately, though. How are you? What are you doing now?
PLATONOV: Fate has played a scurvy trick on me. I could never have foreseen it when you looked on me as a second Byron and I saw myself as a future Cabinet Minister and a Christopher Columbus. I am a schoolmaster, my dear Sophia. That's all.
SOPHIA: You?
PLATONOV: Yes, me . . . (*Pause.*) I admit it's a bit strange . . .
SOPHIA: Incredible! But why? Why not something better than that?
PLATONOV: I'm afraid it needs more than one sentence to answer your question . . . (*Pause.*)
SOPHIA: At least you got your degree, didn't you?
PLATONOV: No.
SOPHIA: I see. Still, this doesn't prevent you from being a man, does it?
PLATONOV: I'm sorry. I didn't quite understand your question.
SOPHIA: I'm afraid I haven't expressed myself quite clearly. What I mean is that this does not prevent you from being a man. I mean, from engaging in some social activities, for example,

women's emancipation, freedom . . . It doesn't stand in your way if you want to devote your time to the service of an idea, does it?

TRILETSKY (*aside*): Talking through her hat!

PLATONOV (*aside*): Good Lord! (*To her.*) Well, how shall I put it? I don't suppose it does, but then . . . why should it? (*He laughs.*) Nothing can stand in my way. You see, I am a big, immovable stone. Big immovable stones have been created for the sole purpose of standing in the way themselves.

Enter SHCHERBUK.

SHCHERBUK (*in the doorway*): Don't give my horses any oats; they pulled badly.

[ANNA: Hurrah! My boy-friend has arrived.

ALL: Good old Paul!

SHCHERBUK (*kisses* Anna's *and* Sasha's *hands in silence, bows to all the men in turn in silence, and then bows to the whole company*): My friends, tell me, unworthy specimen of humanity as I am, where is the woman my heart yearns to see? I suspect, and indeed I am quite convinced, that this woman is—she. (*Points to* Sophia.) Anna, my dear, may I ask you to introduce me to her so that she should know the kind of man I am.]

ANNA (*takes him by the arm and leads him to* Sophia): Paul Shcherbuk, retired Cornet of the Guards.

SHCHERBUK: Is that all?

ANNA: Sorry. Our friend, neighbour, guest and creditor.

SHCHERBUK: Yes, indeed. Our late general's best friend! [Stormed fortresses known to all and sundry as the fair sex under his command.] (*Bows.*) May I kiss your hand, ma'am?

[SOPHIA (*puts out her hand and then pulls it back*): Thank you, but, please, don't.

SHCHERBUK: Deeply hurt, ma'am. Used to carry your husband about in my arms when he was still walking under the table. He left a mark on me, ma'am, a mark I shall carry with me to my grave. (*Opens his mouth.*) Here! No tooth, see? (*Laughter.*) I held him in my arms and he, little Sergey, that is, knocked one of my teeth out with a pistol he happened to be playing about with just then. Reprimanded me by knocking out a tooth. Ha, ha, ha! The naughty boy! Don't stand any nonsense from him, my dear lady, whose name, I regret to say, I haven't the honour of knowing. Your beauty reminds me of a certain picture—er—except that your nose isn't exactly like it . . . Won't you let me kiss your hand, ma'am?

> PETRIN *sits down next to* VENGEROVICH SR. *and reads him something from the paper.*]

SOPHIA (*holding out her hand*): If you insist.

SHCHERBUK (*kisses her hand*): Thank you ma'am. (*To* Platonov.) How are you, my dear chap? Grown into a strapping big fellow, haven't you? (*He sits down.*) [I knew you when you still regarded the world in wonder. Still growing. Yes, you're still growing! Mustn't bring on the evil eye, though. A fellow after my own heart.] Handsome, too! Well, my boy, why don't you join the army?

PLATONOV: I have a weak chest, sir.

SHCHERBUK (*pointing to* Triletsky): Did he tell you that? If you believe that good for nothing quack you'll soon be kicking up daisies.

TRILETSKY: I'll thank you not to call me names, sir.

[SHCHERBUK: Tried to cure my lumbago, he did. Don't eat this, don't eat that. Don't sleep on the floor . . . Well, he damn well didn't cure it. I asked him, Why did you take my money if you didn't cure me? So he says to me, I had to do one of two things, cure you or take your money. What do you make of a fellow like that?

TRILETSKY: Why tell lies, Beelzebub son of Bucephalus? How much money did you give me, may I ask? Try to remember, sir. All I got for six visits was one rouble, a torn one at that. I gave it to a beggar, but he wouldn't take it. It's torn, he said, the serial number's missing.

SHCHERBUK: He paid me six visits not because of my illness but because my tenant's daughter's a tasty bit.

TRILETSKY: Platonov, you're sitting next to him. Land a good blow on his bald pate, there's a good fellow.

SHCHERBUK: Leave me alone. That's enough. Don't tease a sleeping lion. You're still so high! Can hardly see you! (*To* Platonov.) And your father was a fine fellow too! We were great friends, the two of us. A practical joker. We were up to all sorts of devilment, the two of us. Aye, you won't find anyone like him now. Those were the days. (*To* Petrin.) For goodness sake, man, we're talking here and you're reading your paper aloud. Where are your manners?

PETRIN *goes on reading.*]

SASHA (*nudges* Triletsky Sr.): Father, don't fall asleep here! Aren't you ashamed?

[TRILETSKY SR. *wakes up and falls asleep again a minute later.*

SHCHERBUK: No. I can't go on talking! (*He gets up.*) You'd better listen to him ... he's reading.

PETRIN (*gets up and goes over to Platonov*): What did you say, sir?

PLATONOV: I didn't say anything.

PETRIN: You did, sir. You made some remark about me.

PLATONOV: You must have been dreaming.

PETRIN: Making insulting remarks about me, sir?

PLATONOV: I didn't say anything. I assure you, sir. You must have been dreaming.

PETRIN: You can say anything you like ... Petrin ... Petrin ... What about Petrin? (*He puts the paper into his pocket.*) Perhaps Petrin went to a university. He may be a Bachelor of Law. Don't you know that? I shall carry my degree to the grave with me. Yes, sir. A Court Councillor. That's what I am. Didn't you know that? And I have lived a little longer than you. I shall be sixty soon, thank God.

PLATONOV: That's all very nice, but what has it got to do with anything?

PETRIN: Live long enough, my dear fellow, and you'll find out. Life's no joke! Life leaves a nasty mark on you.

PLATONOV: I really don't know what you mean to say by that, sir. I don't understand you. You began telling us all about yourself and now you're going on about life. What has life got to do with you? Have you anything in common?

PETRIN: When life's knocked you about and given you a couple of good jolts, you too can't help looking at the young with a certain circumspection . . . Life, my dear sir . . . What is life? I'll tell you what it is. When a man is born he can choose one of three roads. There are no others. If he takes the road to the right, the wolves will eat him up. If he takes the road to the left, he will eat up the wolves. And if he takes the road straight ahead of him, he'll eat himself up.

PLATONOV: You don't say! Have you come to this world-shattering conclusion by way of science or experience?

PETRIN: By way of experience.

PLATONOV: By way of experience . . . (*Laughs.*) Really, my dear sir, go and tell it to someone else! I'd advise you not to talk of higher things to me. I'm laughing and yet I can scarcely credit it. No, sir, I don't believe in your senile, home-made wisdom. I don't believe, I honestly don't believe, dear friends of my father, in your homely speeches about complicated, abstruse matters. I don't believe in anything you've thought out for yourselves.

PETRIN: I see, sir. Yes, indeed. You can make anything you like of a young tree—a house, a ship, anything you like. But an old, tall, broad tree is no good for anything.

PLATONOV: I was not talking about old men. I was talking about my father's friends.

GLAGOLYEV SR.: I, too, was your father's friend, Michael.

PLATONOV: He had lots of friends . . . The courtyard outside his house used to be crammed full of carriages.

GLAGOLYEV SR.: What I mean is, don't you believe in me, either?

PLATONOV: Well, how shall I put it? No, I don't quite believe in you, either.

GLAGOLYEV SR.: Oh? (*Holds out his hand to him.*) Thank you, my dear fellow, for being so frank with me. Your frankness makes me feel much closer to you.

PLATONOV: You're a good man. I, too, respect you greatly, but . . . but . . .

GLAGOLYEV SR.: Go on.

PLATONOV: But—but one has to be too credulous a man to believe in the Fonvisin characters, the stolid Starodooms and the sugary Milonovs, who spent all their lives eating cabbage soup from the same bowl as the Skotinins and the Prostakovs, and the satraps who're only considered sacred because they do neither good nor evil. Don't be angry with me, please.

ANNA: I don't like this kind of conversation, especially if it's Platonov who is conducting it. They always end badly. Let me introduce our new friend to you, Michael. (*Points to* Vengerovich Jr.) Isaac Vengerovich, a student.

PLATONOV: Oh . . . (*He gets up and walks towards* Vengerovich Jr.) Very pleased to meet you. Very pleased. (*Holds out his hand*). I'd give a lot to have the right to call myself a student now. (*Pause.*) I'm offering you my hand. Take it, or give me yours.

VENGEROVICH JR.: I shall do neither the one nor the other.

PLATONOV: I beg your pardon?

VENGEROVICH JR.: I refuse to shake hands with you.

PLATONOV: A mystery. Why not, sir?

ANNA (*aside*): What on earth! . . .

VENGEROVICH JR.: Because I have a good reason for it. I despise such people as you.

PLATONOV: Jolly good! (*He examines him closely.*) I'd have told you that I was overcome with admiration for you had I not known that it would be too great a sop for your vanity, which must be kept inviolate for future occasions. (*Pause*.) You look at me as a giant might look at a pygmy. Well, perhaps you really are a giant.

VENGEROVICH JR.: I'm an honest man. I'm not a vulgarian.

PLATONOV: On which let me congratulate you. It would indeed have been strange to find that a young student was a dishonest man. No one dreams of questioning your honesty. So you won't shake hands with me, young man?

VENGEROVICH JR.: I'm not a dispenser of charity.

TRILETSKY: Good Lord!

PLATONOV: You won't shake hands with me then. Very well, that's your affair. I was thinking of civility and not of charity. Do you despise me very much?

VENGEROVICH JR.: As much as it is possible for a man who hates vulgarity, spongers, and buffoons.

PLATONOV (*sighs*): I haven't heard such speeches for a long, long time. It takes me back to the days when I was a young student. I, too, was an expert in delivering myself of such compliments. Unfortunately, they're nothing but phrases. Charming phrases, but only phrases. If only there'd been just a little bit of sincerity in them. False notes have a terrible effect on an unaccustomed ear.

VENGEROVICH JR.: Don't you think we'd better put an end to this conversation?

PLATONOV: Why? Our audience seems to be quite enthralled and we haven't as yet reached the point of not being able to stand one another. Come, let's carry on in the same spirit.

VASILY *runs in followed by* OSIP.

OSIP (*enters and clears his throat*): It gives me great pleasure to congratulate your ladyship on your safe return. (*Pause*.) I wish you everything that you wish from God. (*Laughter*.)

PLATONOV: Who do I see? The devil's bosom friend. The terror of the countryside. The most fearsome of mortals.

ANNA: Good gracious, who asked you to come here? You're all we needed! What did you come for?

OSIP: I came to congratulate you, ma'am.

ANNA: I don't want your congratulations. Clear out!

PLATONOV: Is it you who in the darkness of the night and the light of the day fill the hearts of men with terror? It's a long time since I clapped eyes on you, murderer, No. 666! Well, my dear fellow, let's hear you expatiate on something. Let's hearken to the great Osip.]

OSIP (*bows*): Welcome home, your ladyship. (*To* Voynitsev.) And to you, sir. Congratulations on your marriage, sir. God grant that you and your family should prosper, sir!

VOYNITSEV: Thank you. (*To* Sophia.) This, Sophy, is our Voynitsev bugbear.

ANNA: [Don't keep him, Platonov. Let him go. I'm angry with him.] (*To* Osip.) Tell them in the kitchen to give you your dinner. Look at his eyes. The eyes of a wild beast. How much of our timber did you steal last winter?

OSIP (*laughs*): Three or four little trees, perhaps. (*Laughter.*)

ANNA (*laughs*): Liar! I'm sure it's a lot more. Look, he's got a watch chain. How do you like that? Is it a gold one? Tell me what's the time?

OSIP (*looks at the clock*): Twenty-two minutes past one. May I kiss your hand, ma'am?

ANNA (*puts her hand to his lips*): Here, kiss it!

OSIP (*kisses her hand*): Very grateful I am to your ladyship for your sympathy. (*He bows.*) Why are you holding on to me, Mr. Platonov?

PLATONOV: Afraid you might go. I'm very fond of you. What a fine upstanding lad you are, damn you. What on earth made you come here, O wise one!

OSIP: I was running after Vasily and just looked in.

PLATONOV: An intelligent man running after a fool! I have the honour, ladies and gentlemen, to present a most interesting specimen to you. One of the most interesting bloodthirsty animals of our modern zoological museum. (*He turns* Osip *round*.) Known to everyone as Osip. Horsethief, parasite, murderer, and burglar. Born in Voynitsevka, committed all his robberies and murders in Voynitsevka, and always to be found in and around Voynitsevka. (*Laughter*.)

OSIP (*laughs*): You are a caution, sir.

TRILETSKY (*examining* Osip *closely*): What's your trade, my man?

OSIP: Theft, sir.

TRILETSKY: I see. Quite a pleasant occupation. What a cynic you are, though.

OSIP: What's a cynic, sir?

TRILETSKY: A cynic is a Greek word and translated into your language it means a pig who does not care if the whole world knows he is a pig.

PLATONOV: He smiles, ye Gods! What a smile! And his face! Look at his face! Why, there's a ton of brass in that face, You wouldn't break it on a stone so easily. (*Leads* Osip *to a looking glass*.) Look at yourself, monster! See? Aren't you surprised?

OSIP: A most ordinary man, sir. Less, even . . .

PLATONOV: Oh? [Are you sure you're not one of the mythical Russian giants? Not an Ilya Murometz? (*Slaps him on the shoulder*.) Oh, gallant, victorious Russian, what are we compared to thee? Little men, rushing about to and fro, parasites, ignorant of our proper places. Why, you and I should be riding across deserts in the company of other great knights. You and I should be fighting giants with heads as big as mountains, whistling as we perform deeds of derring-do. You would have made short work of the legendary Solovey the Brigand, wouldn't you?

OSIP: I'm sure I don't know, sir.

PLATONOV: Of course you would. Strong, aren't you?] Look at

your muscles. Not muscles but ropes. By the way, why aren't you doing hard labour in Siberia?

ANNA: Stop it, Platonov. It's so boring.

PLATONOV: Haven't you been to prison even once, Osip?

OSIP: Well, sir, as a matter of fact I have . . . Every winter.

PLATONOV: That's how it should be. It's cold in the forest—go to prison. But why aren't you in Siberia?

[OSIP: Don't know, sir. May I go now, sir?

PLATONOV: You don't belong to this world, do you? You're beyond space and time. You're beyond customs and above the law, aren't you?]

OSIP: Well, sir, according to the law you can only be sent to Siberia if you're proved guilty or if you're caught red-handed. Now, sir, I admit that everyone knows I'm a thief and a robber (*laughs*), but not everybody can prove it. You see, sir, the common people have no guts nowadays. They're stupid. Not clever, I mean. They're afraid of everything . . . Afraid of proving anything against me. They could have sent me to Siberia, but they don't know the law. They're terrified of everything. Yes, sir, the common people is an ass, sir. They're always trying to do things behind your back, in a crowd. They're an ignorant, beggarly, scurvy lot, sir. It serves them right if they gets hurt.

PLATONOV: How importantly he talks, the scoundrel. Thought it all out for himself, the disgusting animal, I shouldn't wonder. (*He sighs.*) What abominations are still possible in Russia!

OSIP: I'm not the only one who thinks like that, sir. Everyone thinks like that. Take Mr. Vengerovich here, for instance.

PLATONOV: Yes, but he, too, is above the law. Everyone knows, but not everyone can prove it.

VENGEROVICH SR.: I suggest you leave me out of it.

PLATONOV: It's no use talking about him. He's been made in your image but he's cleverer than you. [That's the difference and that's why he's as happy as an Arcadian shepherd. It isn't quite safe to tell him what he is to his face, but one can tell you.] You're birds of a feather, but . . . he owns sixty pubs, my dear fellow, sixty pubs. You haven't even got sixty copecks.

VENGEROVICH SR.: Sixty-three pubs.

PLATONOV: He'll have seventy-three next year. He contributes to public charities, he gives public dinners, he is a respected member of society, everyone bows and scrapes to him. You too are a great man, but you don't know how to live. You don't know how to live, you bad man.

VENGEROVICH SR.: You're letting your imagination run away with you, my dear sir. (*He gets up and sits down on another chair.*)

PLATONOV: There are more lightning conductors on that head. He'll live as long as he's lived already, if not more, and, damn him, he'll die in peace.

ANNA: Stop it, Platonov!

VOYNITSEV: Calm down, my dear chap. Osip, you'd better go. You're only exasperating Platonov by your presence.

VENGEROVICH SR.: He wants to turn me out of here, but he won't succeed.

PLATONOV: I will. I will succeed. If not, I'll go myself.

ANNA: For heaven's sake, will you stop, Platonov? Don't make speeches. Just tell me, are you going to stop or not?

SASHA: Shut up for goodness' sake! (*Softly.*) It isn't nice. You're embarrassing me.

PLATONOV (*to* Osip): Clear out! Hope you'll disappear from here soon—and for good!

OSIP: Marfa Petrovna has a talking parrot. It calls men and dogs fools, but when it catches sight of a vulture or of Mr. Vengerovich it screeches, 'Damn you!' (*He bursts out laughing.*) Goodbye, ladies and gentlemen. (*He goes out.*)

VENGEROVICH SR.: If I'm to be lectured on morals, it's not going to be by you, young man, and certainly not in such a manner. I'm a citizen, and to be quite truthful, a useful citizen. I'm a father. And what are you? What are you, young man? You are, I'm sorry to say, a good-for-nothing spendthrift, a landowner who has squandered his fortune, a man who is devoid of all moral sense and is not fit for the important job he has undertaken.

PLATONOV: A citizen ... If you're a citizen, then the word citizen isn't a nice word. It's a dirty word!

ANNA: He just won't stop! Why do you spoil the day for us with your preaching, Platonov? Why talk about things that are best left alone? And, besides, what right have you to talk about them?

TRILETSKY: You can never feel comfortable with these most just and most honest men. They never leave things alone, they always interfere, everything is their business.

GLAGOLYEV SR.: Gentlemen, you haven't come here to call each other names.

ANNA: Nor should you, Platonov, forget that visitors who start quarrelling put their hosts in a very awkward position.

VOYNITSEV: That's quite true. And therefore let there be complete silence from this very minute. Peace, harmony, silence.

VENGEROVICH SR.: He won't leave me in peace for a moment. What have I done to him? The charlatan!

VOYNITSEV: Shhhh!

TRILETSKY: Let them call each other names. What do we care?

Pause.

PLATONOV: [Every time you look around you and consider things seriously, it's enough to make you give up the ghost. And what's so awful is that everyone who's just a little honest and decent keeps silent, dead silent, and merely looks on ...] Everyone looks at him with fear. Everyone prostrates himself to this obese upstart just because he's rolling in money! Everyone owes him money. Honour's flown out the window.

ANNA: Do be quiet, Platonov! You're starting last year's business all over again and you know I can't bear it.

PLATONOV (*taking a drink of water*): All right. (*He sits down.*)

VENGEROVICH SR.: All right. (*Pause.*)
[SHCHERBUK: I am a martyr, my friends, a real martyr.
ANNA: What next?
SHCHERBUK: I'm in a devil of a mess, my friends. I'd much rather be dead than go on living with a malicious wife. We had a hell of a row again. She nearly killed me a week ago with that devil, that red-haired Don Juan of hers. I was peacefully asleep in the yard under an apple tree, dreaming happily, and looking with regret at the pictures of my past as they unrolled themselves before my mind's eye. (*He sighs.*) Suddenly—suddenly someone hit me a terrific blow on the head. Good Lord! I thought my end had come. An earthquake, a battle of the elements, a flood, a rain of fire. I opened my eyes and there he stood before me, the red-haired fellow! Caught me by the shoulder, began raining blows on me, and flung me to the ground. Then that fury leapt on top of me, seized me by my innocent beard (*grasping his beard*). It was no joke. (*He slaps himself on his bald head.*) They nearly killed me. I honestly thought my end had come.
ANNA: You're exaggerating, surely.
SHCHERBUK: My wife's an old hag, ugly as sin, and she is in love too, if you please ... The old witch! And, of course, that's just what the red-haired fellow wants. It's money he needs, you see, and not her love.]

YAKOV *comes in and hands a visiting card to* ANNA.

VOYNITSEV: Who's this from?
ANNA [(*to* Shcherbuk): Do be quiet, Paul.] (*Reads.*) Le Comte Glagolief. Why all this ceremony? Ask him to come in, please. (*To* Glagolyev Sr.) It's your son.
GLAGOLYEV SR.: My son? Where has he sprung from? He's supposed to be abroad.

GLAGOLYEV JR. *enters.*

ANNA: My dear Cyril. How nice to see you!

GLAGOLYEV SR. (*gets up*): When did you arrive, Cyril? (*He sits down.*)
GLAGOLYEV JR.: How do you do, ladies and gentlemen? [Platonov, Vengerovich, Triletsky—how are you? I see our eccentric Platonov is here, too. Greetings to everyone.] It's so frightfully hot in Russia. I've come straight from Paris, straight from France. Phew! You don't believe me? My word of honour. Only stopped for a minute at home to leave my trunk. Well, ladies and gentlemen, Paris is quite a city!
VOYNITSEV: Sit down, Frenchman.
GLAGOLYEV JR.: No, thank you. I haven't come visiting, I just want to ... er ... I mean, I just want to see my father for a minute. (*To his father.*) Now really, look here, father ...
GLAGOLYEV SR.: What's the matter?
GLAGOLYEV JR.: You don't want to pick a quarrel with me, do you? Why didn't you send me money when I asked you to?
GLAGOLYEV SR.: We'll talk about it at home.
GLAGOLYEV JR.: Why *didn't* you send me any money? You laugh? You think it's a joke, do you? Everything's a joke to you. Ladies and gentlemen, can one live abroad without money?
ANNA: What's life in Paris like? Do sit down, Cyril.
GLAGOLYEV JR.: Because of him I came back with nothing but my toothbrush. I sent him thirty-five telegrams from Paris. Why didn't you send me any money, I ask you? Blushing? Ashamed, are you?
TRILETSKY: Do not shout, my lord. If you go on shouting, I shall send your visiting card to our local magistrate and charge you with the wrongful assumption of a count's title. It's indecent.
GLAGOLYEV SR.: Don't make a scene, Cyril. I thought that six thousand would be enough. Calm down, please.
GLAGOLYEV JR.: Give me the money and I'll go back to France at once. Give it me this minute. This minute! [I'm off! Give it me at once.] I'm in a hurry.

ANNA: Why all this hurry? There's plenty of time. You'd better tell us something about your travels.

YAKOV (*comes in*): Lunch is served.

ANNA: Thank you. In that case, ladies and gentlemen, let's go and eat.

TRILETSKY: Eat? Hurrah! (*He seizes* Sasha's *arm with one hand and* Cyril Glagolyev's *with the other and runs.*)

SASHA: Let go, you idiot! I'll go by myself.

GLAGOLYEV JR.: Let go! What boorishness! I don't like jokes! (*He frees himself.*)

SASHA *and* TRILETSKY *run out of the room.*

ANNA (*takes* Cyril Glagolyev's *arm*): Come along, Parisian. It's no use losing your temper for nothing. (*To* Vengerovich *and* Bugrov.) Come, gentlemen. (*She goes out with* Cyril Glagolyev.)

BUGROV (*gets up and stretches himself*): You could starve to death before you got your lunch here. (*He goes out.*)

PLATONOV (*offers* Sophia *his arm*): May I? Don't look so astonished! This is still an unknown world to you. This, Sophia, is a world (*lowering his voice*) of fools, utter, hopeless fools. (*He goes out with* Sophia.)

[VENGEROVICH SR. (*to his son*): Now you've seen him, haven't you?

VENGEROVICH JR.: A most original scoundrel. (*He goes out with his father.*)]

VOYNITSEV (*nudges* Col. Triletsky): Come on, sir! Lunch!

COL. TRILETSKY (*jumps up*): Eh? Who?

VOYNITSEV: No one. Let's go and have lunch.

COL. TRILETSKY: Very good, my dear chap. (*He goes out with* Voynitsev *and* Shcherbuk.)

[PETRIN: You'd like it, wouldn't you?

GLAGOLYEV SR.: I don't mind. I've told you already.]

PETRIN (*to* Glagolyev Sr.): Have you made up your mind to get married?

GLAGOLYEV SR.: I don't know. The question is, will she marry me?

PETRIN: Of course she will. I'm quite sure she will.

GLAGOLYEV SR.: Who can tell? It isn't the sort of thing one can be sure about. [You can never tell what's at the back of the mind of another person.] But why are you so anxious about it?

PETRIN: Why, my dear sir, who else but you should I be anxious about? You're a good man, she's a nice woman. If you like, I'll have a talk to her.

GLAGOLYEV SR.: I'll talk to her myself. Don't say anything for the time being, and—please, if you possibly can, don't be so anxious about me. I'm quite capable of getting married myself. (*He goes out.*)

PETRIN (*alone*): If only he could! Holy saints, put yourselves in my place. If the widow marries him, I'm a rich man. I shall get cash for my bills of exchange, dear saints. Even my appetite's gone at this happy thought. [Thy servants Anna and Porfiry, I mean, Porfiry and Anna are about to pledge their troth . . .]

ANNA *enters.*

ANNA: Why aren't you going in to lunch?

PETRIN: My dear lady, may I drop a hint?

ANNA: By all means, only be quick about it. I'm in a hurry.

PETRIN: Well, can you let me have a little money, my dear lady?

ANNA: A hint? It's more like a demand. How much do you want? One rouble? Two roubles?

PETRIN: Won't you honour at least a few of your bills of exchange? I'm sick and tired of looking at them. A bill of exchange is nothing but a mirage, a daydream. They say to you, 'You're rich.' But the plain fact is that you're anything but rich.

ANNA: Are you still talking about the sixteen thousand roubles? Aren't you ashamed? [Don't you wince when asking for the repayment of that loan? Really sir!] What does an old bachelor like you want that ill-gotten money for?

PETRIN: What do I want it for? Why, my dear lady, it belongs to me.

ANNA: You swindled my husband out of that money when he was drunk and ill. Don't you remember that?

PETRIN: What has that got to do with it, my dear lady? They are bills of exchange, aren't they? And bills of exchange have to be paid. An account has to be settled.

ANNA: [All right, all right. That's enough.] I have no money and I shall never have it for people like you. Go and present your bills of exchange. A Bachelor of Law, too! Why, you'll be dead soon. Why are you trying to swindle me? [What a funny fellow you are!]

PETRIN: May I drop a hint, my dear lady?

ANNA: You may not, sir! (*She goes towards the door.*) Go and eat.

PETRIN: One moment, please, dear lady. One moment. Do you like Porfiry?

ANNA: Mind your own business, sir. What right have you to meddle in mine. Bachelor of Law, indeed!

PETRIN: What right? (*Beating his breast.*) And who, may I ask, was the late Major General's best friend? Who closed his eyes on his death bed?

ANNA: You, you, you! [You did well and] I shall always be grateful to you for it.

PETRIN: Well, I suppose I'd better go and drink to his memory. (*He sighs.*) And to your health! You're a proud and haughty woman, my dear lady. Pride is a vice, ma'am. (*He goes out.*)

PLATONOV *enters.*

PLATONOV: The self-conceit of the man, damn him! You tell him to clear out, and he sits there as if nothing were happening! [The self-conceit of a born oaf and money grubber.] A penny for your thoughts, your ladyship.

ANNA: Have you calmed down?

PLATONOV: I have. Don't let's be cross. (*He kisses her hand.*) Every one of them ought to be driven out of your house.

ANNA: Oh, if only, my dear, insufferable Platonov, I could drive them all out! You can't imagine how happy that would make me. But, the trouble is, you see, that the honour you were so eloquent about for my benefit today is applicable only in theory and not in practice. I have no right to drive them out, and neither have you with all your eloquence. For, you see, they are our benefactors, our creditors. I've only to look askance at them and the very next day we shall be evicted. As you see, it's either honour or the estate. I choose the estate. Make whatever you like of it, my dear windbag, but if you don't want me to leave this beautiful place, don't remind me of honour and don't insult my geese . . . They're calling me . . . We're going for a drive after dinner. Don't you dare leave. (*She slaps him on the shoulder.*) We're going to have a lovely time! Come on, let's eat. (*She goes out.*)

[PLATONOV (*after a pause*): I'm going to drive him out all the same. I'll drive them all out. It may be stupid and tactless but I'm going to do it. I promised myself to have nothing to do with the swine, but I'm afraid I can't help it. A strong character is uncontrollable, and a weak one all the more so.

VENGEROVICH JR. *enters.*

VENGEROVICH JR.: Look here, Mr. Schoolmaster, I'd advise you to leave my father alone.
PLATONOV: Thanks for your advice.
VENGEROVICH JR. I'm not joking. My father knows many influential people, and he can easily get you the sack. I warn you.
PLATONOV: Most magnanimous, young man. What's your name?
VENGEROVICH JR.: Isaac.
PLATONOV: So Abraham begat Isaac. Thank you, magnanimous young man. Will you, in turn, be so good as to tell your dear father that I wish that he and many like him would go to blazes. Go and eat, young man, they'll eat everything up.
VENGEROVICH JR. (*shrugging and going towards the door*): It would

be funny if it were not so stupid. (*Stopping.*) Don't think I'm angry with you because you don't let my father alone. Not in the least. I'm merely interested in finding out what people are really like. I'm not at all angry. By making a study of you, I'm trying to find out what our modern Chatskys are like. I understand you only too well. If you had been happy, if you hadn't been so bored with doing nothing, it would never have occurred to you to worry my father. You, Mr. Chatsky, are not looking for justice, you're merely amusing yourselves, enjoying yourselves. Now that you've no longer any menials you have to abuse someone. So you abuse everybody who happens to cross your path.

PLATONOV (*laughs*): That's lovely! And, you know, you, too, have just a little reason of your own for —abusing people.

VENGEROVICH JR.: What is so remarkable is the revolting fact that you never quarrel with my father when you're alone with him. You choose a drawing-room for your diversions, for there the fools can see you in all your glory. Oh, you theatrical fellow!

PLATONOV: I'd like to have a talk with you in ten years' time, or even five. What will you be like then? Will this tone of voice, these flashing eyes, be the same? No, young man, you're sure to deteriorate. And how are your university studies getting along? I can see from the expresssion on your face that they're not getting along at all well. You will deteriorate! However, go and eat. I'm not going to talk to you any more. I don't like your spiteful face.

VENGEROVICH JR. (*laughs*): An asthete! (*He goes towards the door.*) I'd rather have a spiteful face than one that asks to be slapped.

PLATONOV: Quite. But—go and eat.

VENGEROVICH JR.: We don't know one another. Don't forget that, please. (*He goes out.*)

PLATONOV (*alone*): Ignorant young idiot! Thinks a lot and talks a lot—behind your back.] (*Looking through the door into the dining-room.*) Looking for me with those velvety eyes of hers.

How very pretty she still is! There's so much beauty in her face. Her hair is the same. Same colour, same style. How many times have I kissed that hair! How many wonderful memories that pretty head of hers brings back to me!... (*Pause.*) Has the time come for me, too, to be satisfied with memories? (*Pause.*) There's nothing wrong with memories but—is it really the end? Oh, God forbid, God forbid! I'd rather be dead. I must live. I must live. I'm still young!

VOYNITSEV *enters*.

VOYNITSEV (*wiping his lips with his napkin*): Come, let's drink to Sophia's health. What are you hiding for? Well?

PLATONOV: I keep looking at your wife. Can't help admiring her. [What a paragon of a wife!]

VOYNITSEV (*laughs*).

PLATONOV: You're a lucky devil.

VOYNITSEV: Yes. You're right. I am lucky. Well, not actually... I mean... er... I can't honestly say that I'm absolutely... er ... but on the whole I suppose I am.

PLATONOV (*looking through the door into the dining-room*): I've known her a long time. [I know her like the back of my hand.] She's very beautiful but—oh!—she used to be much more beautiful! Pity you didn't know her then. She *is* beautiful, though.

VOYNITSEV: Indeed she is.

PLATONOV: Her eyes!

VOYNITSEV: And her hair?

PLATONOV: Oh, she was such a wonderful girl! (*He laughs.*) But look at my Sasha! A peasant girl. There she sits. You can just see her behind the decanter of vodka. Flustered, worried, terribly indignant at my behaviour. Worried to death, poor thing, at the thought that everyone now hates and condemns me for my quarrel with Vengerovich.

VOYNITSEV: Excuse a personal question—are you happy with her?

PLATONOV: It's the family, my dear fellow. Take my family away from me and I believe I'd be utterly lost. A home . . . After a while you, too, will find out. [Pity you have sown so few wild oats. You don't appreciate the value of a family.] I wouldn't sell my plain Sasha for a million. We get on marvellously together. She's a fool, and I'm a failure.

TRILETSKY *comes in*.

PLATONOV (*to* Triletsky): Full up?

TRILETSKY: Very much so. (*He slaps himself on the stomach.*) Hard as a drum. Come on, we must drink to the safe arrival of our travellers. Oh, my dear fellows . . . (*He embraces them both.*) Come, let's drink to their health! [Lord! (*He stretches himself.*) What's the life of a man worth! Blessed is he that does not hearken to the counsel of the unrighteous. (*He stretches himself.*) Oh, you silly fools, you dirty rascals!]

PLATONOV: Been visiting your patients today?

TRILETSKY: Later, later. Now, look here, Michael. I'm telling you once and for all: leave me be. I'm sick and tired of your sermons. Why don't you try to love humanity for a change? Can't you get it into your head that you're the last man on earth to make any impression on me? [But, of course, if you can't help it, if your tongue itches to say what you think of me, then put it all down in writing, dear boy. I promise you I'll learn it all by heart. Or read me your sermon at a specially appointed hour. I'm willing to give you one hour a day—er—from four to five in the afternoon, for instance. All right? I'm even willing to pay you a rouble for that hour.] (*He stretches himself.*) All day long, all day long!

PLATONOV (*to* Voynitsev): Please explain to me the meaning of that advertisement in the newspaper. Has it really come to that?

VOYNITSEV: No, no. Don't worry. (*He laughs.*) It's just a little business arrangement. There'll be a public auction and Glagolyev will buy our estate. He'll free us from our obligations to the bank and we'll pay him the interest on the mortgage. It was his idea.

PLATONOV: I don't understand. What does he get out of it? He's not making you a present of the estate, is he? It's an odd kind of present and—er—I don't think you need it at all.

VOYNITSEV: Well, no . . . As a matter of fact, I don't quite understand it myself. Ask mother, she'll explain it to you. All I know is that after the sale, the estate will still be ours and that we shall pay the mortgage off to Glagolyev in instalments. Mother will give him her five thousand as a deposit. Anyway, it will be much more convenient to deal with him than with the bank. You can't imagine how sick and tired I am of that bank. [I assure you, you're not as tired of Triletsky as I am of that bank.] But enough of business. (*Taking* Platonov *by the arm.*) Come, let's drink to our friendship, dear friends. I don't mind if I lose everything, if all these business arrangements come to nothing, provided the people I love—you, my Sonia, and my stepmother—are well and happy. You are all I care for in life. Come on!

PLATONOV: I'm coming. I shall drink to it all and I expect I shall drink it all. I haven't been drunk for a long time, and I'm dying to get really drunk.

ANNA (*in the doorway*): Perfect friendship! A fine troika! (*She sings.*) Shall I harness a troika of swift . . .

TRILETSKY: . . . dark-brown steeds . . . Let's start with the brandy my dear fellows!

ANNA (*at the door*): Run along, parasites! Go and eat. Everything's gone cold.

PLATONOV: Perfect friendship! I hope, my dear friends, you won't have to weep because of my friendship. Let's drink to the happy ending of all friendships, including ours. May its end be as untempestuous and as imperceptible as its beginning. (*He goes out into the dining-room.*)

END OF ACT ONE

ACT TWO

SCENE ONE

The garden. In the foreground, a flower-bed with a path running round it. In the middle of the flower-bed a statue with a lampion on top. Benches, chairs, and small tables. To the right, the façade of the house. Front steps leading to its entrance. The windows are open. From the windows come the sounds of laughter, conversation, and a piano and a violin playing quadrilles, waltzes, etc. At the back of the garden, a pagoda festooned with lanterns. Over the entrance to the pagoda, a monogram with the letters 'S.V.' Behind the pagoda, people can be heard playing skittles, the sound of the rolling balls and shouts of 'Five down! Four left!' House and garden are illuminated. Guests and servants are walking to and fro. VASILY *and* YAKOV *(in tails, and both of them drunk) are hanging up lanterns and lighting lampions.*

BUGROV *and* TRILETSKY (TRILETSKY *in a peaked hat with a cockade*) *come up to the house arm in arm.*

TRILETSKY: Come on, out with it! It's nothing to you. I'm only asking for a loan.

BUGROV: I'm sorry, I can't. Please don't insist, doctor.

TRILETSKY: Of course you can. You can do everything. You can buy up the whole universe thrice over, only you don't want to. All I ask is for a loan. A loan, I tell you, you funny fellow. I swear you won't get it back.

BUGROV: Ah, you see, you see? Let the cat out of the bag, haven't you?

TRILETSKY: I don't see anything. All I see is that you are an unfeeling brute. Come on, let me have it, great man. [No? Let's have it, please.] I beg. I implore. Are you really such an unfeeling brute? Have you no heart?

BUGROV (*sighs*): Dear, oh dear . . . You don't cure the sick, but you will have their money.

TRILETSKY: Well said. (*He sighs.*) I suppose you're right.

BUGROV (*takes out his wallet*): And the way you make fun of people, doctor. The smallest trifle, and you—ha, ha, ha! It isn't nice, is it? I should think not. We may not be educated, but we're all baptized, same as you scholars. If I say something silly, you ought to correct me and not laugh . . . Yes, sir. We're just peasants, sir. Ordinary peasants. You can't expect much from us. So you must bear with us. (*He opens his wallet.*) For the last time, sir. (*He counts.*) One, six, twelve.

TRILETSKY (*peeps into the wallet*): Good Lord! And they say the Russians haven't any money. Where did you collect it all?

BUGROV: Fifty. (*He gives him the money.*) For the last time.

TRILETSKY: And what's that note in there? Come, let's have it, too. It looks at me so enticingly. (*Taking the money.*) Let's have that note, too, there's a good chap.

BUGROV (*gives him the note*): Take it, sir. I'm afraid you're a little too greedy, doctor.

TRILETSKY: [All in one rouble notes. You haven't been begging in the streets, have you? They're not forged by any chance, are they?

BUGROV: Let me have them back if you think they're forged.

TRILETSKY: I'd gladly give them back if I thought you needed them. Thanks, my dear fellow. I hope you get fatter and are given a medal. Tell me, Bugrov, why do you lead such an abnormal life? You drink a lot, you talk in a deep voice, you sweat, you don't sleep when you ought to. Why aren't you asleep now, for instance? You're a full-blooded fellow, temperamental, easily roused. You ought to go to bed early. You've got more veins than any other man. You mustn't go on killing yourself, must you?

BUGROV: Are you serious, sir?

TRILETSKY: Serious? Of course I'm serious. However, don't be scared. I'm joking. It's too soon for you to die. You'll live a long time yet. Have you got a lot of money, my dear fellow?

BUGROV: Enough to last me my lifetime.

TRILETSKY: You're a good, clever man, Bugrov, but a great scoundrel. I'm sorry, but I'm just talking to you as a friend. We are friends, aren't we? A great scoundrel!] Why are you buying up Voynitsev's bills of exchange? Why are you lending him money?

BUGROV: That's something you wouldn't understand, sir.

TRILETSKY: Want to lay your greedy hands on the Voynitsev mines, don't you? You and Vengerovich. The general's widow won't let her stepson go bankrupt and she'll give you her mines. That's what you're counting on, isn't it? You're a great man, but a scoundrel. A dirty rogue!

BUGROV: Look here, sir, I'll go and take a nap somewhere near the summer house. Please, wake me when they start serving supper.

TRILETSKY: Excellent. Go and sleep.

BUGROV [(*going*)]: And if they don't serve any supper, wake me at half past ten. (*He*) *walks off towards the pagoda.*)

TRILETSKY (*examining the money*): Smells of peasant. Must have been robbing people right and left, the rogue. Where can I put them? (*To* Vasily *and* Yakov.) Hey, you two hired slaves! Vasily, tell Yakov to come here. Come on, you two! Shake a leg!

YAKOV *and* VASILY *walk up to* TRILETSKY.

TRILETSKY: In tails! Damn it all! You certainly look uncommonly like your masters. (*Gives* Yakov *a rouble*.) There's a rouble for you. (*To* Vasily.) And there's a rouble for you. That's because you have long noses, both of you.

VASILY and YAKOV (*bowing*): Thank you very much, sir.

TRILETSKY: [Reeling, are you, Slavs? Drunk? Drunk as lords, both of you. You'll catch it from the mistress when she finds out. She'll box your ears, she will. (*He gives them another rouble each.*)] There's another rouble each for you. That's because your name's Vasily and yours Yakov and not the other way round. Bow!

YAKOV *and* VASILY *bow*.

TRILETSKY: That's right. And there's another rouble each for you because my name's Nicholas and not Ivan. (*He gives them more money.*) Come on, bow! That's right. [Mind, do not spend it on drink. I'll prescribe a nasty medicine for you if you do.] You're terribly like your masters! Go and light the lanterns! At the double! I've had enough of you.

YAKOV *and* VASILY *walk off.* VOYNITSEV *walks across the stage.*

TRILETSKY (*to* Voynitsev): Here you are, three roubles for you!

VOYNITSEV *takes the money, puts it absent-mindedly in his pocket and walks off into the garden.*

TRILETSKY: Say thank you, at least!

COL. TRILETSKY *and* SASHA *come out of the house.*

SASHA (*entering*): Goodness, when will it all end? Dear God, why have you punished me so? Father's drunk, Nicholas is drunk, Michael is drunk. Have you no fear of God, you wretches, if you are not ashamed before men? They're all looking at you. What do you think I feel like when everyone's pointing at you?

[COL. TRILETSKY: No, no, that's not it. Wait, you're confusing me. Wait!

SASHA: You oughtn't to be let into a decent house. You're no sooner in than you're drunk. Oh, you're awful! An old man, too. You ought to set an example to them and not drink with them.

COL. TRILETSKY: Wait, wait! You've got me all confused. What was I talking about? Oh, yes! Damn it all, Sasha, I'm not lying. Another five years in the army, and I'd be a general. You don't think so? (*Laughing at the top of his voice.*) A man like me—and not be a general? With my education? You don't understand a damn thing if you think that. You don't understand a damn thing.

SASHA: Come along! Generals don't drink like that.

COL. TRILETSKY: Everybody drinks when he's feeling happy. Yes, I would have been a general. Shut up, for goodness sake! Just like that mother of yours. Yackety-yak. Why, she'd go on and on, day and night, day and night. One thing isn't right, another isn't right. On and on. What was I talking about? Oh, yes. You're just like your mother. Just like her. Same eyes, same hair... And the way you walk is like her too. Like a little goose. (*He kisses her.*) My angel! Just like your dear mother. Oh, how I loved her, your dear mother.

SASHA: Don't go on like this, father! Come along! Seriously, father, it's time you gave up drinking and making a public exhibition of yourself. Leave it to those two big boys. They're young. It really doesn't suit an old man like you.

COL. TRILETSKY: Of course, of course, my dear, I understand. Won't do it again. Yes, yes, yes, of course, I understand... What was I talking about?

TRILETSKY (*to his father*): Here's a hundred copecks for you, sir. (*He gives him a rouble.*)

COL. TRILETSKY: Thank you, thank you, my son. Yes, indeed, I wouldn't take it from a stranger, but always from a son of mine. Take it, and thank the Lord for it. Don't like other people's money, my children. Don't like it at all. I'm an honest man. Your father's an honest man. Never robbed my country or my children. Damn easy it was too. All I had to do was to put my hand in the right place and I'd have been rich and famous.

TRILETSKY: That's very commendable, father, but you mustn't boast about it.

COL. TRILETSKY: I'm not boasting, Nicholas. I'm merely giving you a piece of advice. Trying to get some sense into your heads. You see, I shall have to answer to God for you.

TRILETSKY: Where are you off to?

COL. TRILETSKY: Home. Just seeing this little chatter-box home. 'Take me home, take me home!' She kept pestering me. So I'm taking her home and then I'll come back.

TRILETSKY: Of course, come back.] (*To* Sasha.) Would you like some money too? Here's some for you, and some for you, Father—three roubles each.

SASHA: Give me another two, please. I'll buy Michael another pair of summer trousers. There's nothing worse than having only one pair. He has to wear his cotton trousers when I'm washing his summer ones.

TRILETSKY: If I had any say in the matter I wouldn't give him any. Let him walk about without. But what am I to do with you? Here, there's two more roubles for you. (*He gives her the money*.)

[COL. TRILETSKY: What was I talking about? Oh yes. I can remember it as if it happened yesterday. I was attached to the G.H.Q. Fought the enemy with my brains. Shed Turkish blood with my wits. Never knew what a bayonet was for, never. Well, yes...

SASHA: What are we standing here for? Let's go. Good-bye Nicholas. Come along, father.

COL. TRILETSKY: Wait! Shut up for God's sake! Yackety-yak. Chattering away like a damn magpie. Now, that's the way to live, children. Honestly, honourably, without a stain on your character. Yes, indeed. Was awarded the Cross of St. Vladimir, third class...

SASHA: That's enough, father, come along!

TRILETSKY: We know the sort of man you are, father, without you making speeches about it. Run along, see her home.]

COL. TRILETSKY: You're a most intelligent fellow, Nicholas. You'll be a great doctor one day. A second Pirogov.

TRILETSKY: Run along.

COL. TRILETSKY: What was I talking about? Oh, yes. I met Pirogov once. I was stationed in Kiev at the time. Yes, yes. Oh, damn clever chap, damn clever. Friendly, too. Well, yes, so I suppose I'd better be going along. Come along, Sasha, my dear. Afraid, children, I'm getting very feeble, tottering on the edge of the grave. Dear Lord, forgive us, sinners that we are! We have sinned! Yes, indeed. I've sinned, children, I've sinned. Now I am serving Mammon and as a young man I never said my prayers. Always made a hell of a noise. [Matter! *Stoff und Kraft*. Oh, dear Lord. Well, yes. Pray, children, that I shouldn't die.] Have you gone, Sasha, my dear? Where are you? Oh, there you are! Come along!

ANNA *looks out of the window.*

[TRILETSKY: Still here? He's talking a lot of nonsense, poor old fellow. Well? Why, don't you go? Remember, don't go past the water mill, the dogs will tear you to pieces there.

SASHA: You're wearing his cap, Nicholas. Give it to him or he'll catch a cold.

TRILETSKY (*takes off the cap and puts it on his father's head*): Onward, old man. Left turn, march!

COL. TRILETSKY: L-l-e-e-ft i-in-cli-i-ne! Yes, yes, you're quite right, Nicholas. God knows, you are. And Michael's quite right, too. He's a freethinker, but he's right. Coming, coming . . . (*They are going off.*) Come on, Sasha. Come, let me carry you.

SASHA: Don't be silly, father.

COL. TRILETSKY: Come, let me carry you. I always used to carry your mother. Carried her about, swaying from side to side. Once came crashing down a little hill with her. She just laughed, the darling. Wasn't a bit angry. Come, let me carry you.

SASHA: Don't talk nonsense! Put your cap on properly. (*She straightens his cap.*) You're such a fine fellow still, father.
COL. TRILETSKY: Yes, yes.] (*They go out.*)

Enter PETRIN *and* SHCHERBUK

PETRIN (*comes out of the house arm in arm with* Shcherbuk): Put fifty thousand in front of me and I'd take them. On my word of honour, I would. Always provided, of course, that I was not caught. Yes sir, I'd take them all right. Put them in front of you and you'd take them too.

SHCHERBUK: I wouldn't, my dear sir, I certainly wouldn't.

PETRIN: Put a rouble in front of me and I'd take that too. Honestly! Good Lord, who wants your honesty? An honest man is only another word for a fool.

SHCHERBUK: I am a fool then. I don't care.

TRILETSKY: Here you are, you wise old men, a rouble for each of you. (*He gives them a rouble each.*)

PETRIN (*taking the money*): Thanks.

SHCHERBUK (*bursts out laughing and takes the money*): Many thanks, doctor.

[TRILETSKY: Filled your bellies, gentlemen?
PETRIN: A little.]

TRILETSKY: And here's another rouble for each of you for a requiem mass for your souls. You've plenty of sins, both of you, haven't you? Well, take the money. All you deserve is a fig each but, hang it all, I'll be generous for once. It's a festive occasion, after all.

ANNA (*at the window*): Triletsky, give me a rouble. (*She disappears.*)

TRILETSKY: For the widow of a Major-General one rouble isn't enough. I'll give you five roubles. One moment. (*He goes into the house.*)

PETRIN (*looks at the window*): So the fairy princess has disappeared, has she?

SHCHERBUK (*looks at the window*): Yes.

PETRIN: Can't stand her. A bad woman. Too proud. A woman must be gentle and respectful. (*He shakes his head.*) Seen Glagolyev? There's another stuffed-shirt for you. Sits there like a mushroom without stirring from his place. Never says a word. Just stares. Is that the way to pay court to a lady?

SHCHERBUK: He'll marry her.

PETRIN: When? In a hundred years? Thank you very much. In a hundred years it won't be any use to me.

SHCHERBUK: As a matter of fact, my dear sir, an old man like him shouldn't marry at all. [If he does, I mean if he really wants to badly, he ought to marry some old fool.] He's no good for her. She's young, fiery, a European lady, well educated.

PETRIN: Oh, if only he would marry her! I want this marriage more than I can say. You see, after the death of the general, may he rest in peace, they haven't a penny left. Not a penny. She owns mines, but then Vengerovich has an eye on them. How can I compete with Vengerovich? How much could I get on their bills of exchange now? I mean if I was to present them today, what can I hope to get for them?

SHCHERBUK: *Nihil.*

PETRIN: But if she married Glagolyev, I should know who to get it from. I'd present the bills of exchange immediately and take out an order of distraint. She won't let her stepson go bankrupt. She'll pay up. Dear, oh dear, I'm afraid it's just a dream, but how I wish it would come true. Sixteen thousand, my dear fellow!

SHCHERBUK: Of which three thousand are mine. [That old hag of a wife of mine is screaming for the money. You must get it, you must get it!] But how am I to get it? They are not peasants. They are my friends. [Let her try and get it herself.] Come on, old man, let's go to the servants' quarters.

PETRIN: What for?

SHCHERBUK: To whisper sweet nothings to the girls.

PETRIN: Is Dunyasha there?

SHCHERBUK: She's there. (*They go.*) It's more fun there. (*Sings.*) Oh, how unhappy I am now that she is far away.

PETRIN: Tick-tock, tick-tock. (*Shouts.*) Yes, sir. (*Sings.*) Merrily the new year we'll meet in true friends' company.

VOYNITSEV and SOPHIA emerge from the back of the garden.

VOYNITSEV: What are you thinking of, Sophia?

SOPHIA: I'm sure I don't know.

VOYNITSEV: You won't let me help you . . . [Don't you think I could?] Why all these secrets, Sophy? Secrets from your husband . . . (*They sit down.*)

SOPHIA: What secrets? I don't know myself what's going on inside me. Please, don't torture me without any reason, Sergey. Don't pay any attention to my black moods. (*Pause.*) Let's go away from here, Sergey.

VOYNITSEV: Away from here?

SOPHIA: Yes.

VOYNITSEV: Why?

SOPHIA: I want to. Let's go abroad. Shall we?

VOYNITSEV: If you insist. But why?

SOPHIA: It's nice here, the air's wholesome, the people are cheerful, but I—I can't . . . Everything seems to be all right, but—we must go away. You promised me not to ask any questions.

VOYNITSEV: We shall leave tomorrow. [I promise you we won't be here tomorrow.] (*He kisses her hand.*) You must be awfully bored here. Well, [I can understand that.] I realize how you must feel. Such horrible people! The Petrins, the Shcherbuks.

SOPHIA: They have nothing to do with it. Don't let's talk about them. (*Pause.*)

VOYNITSEV: Why are you women always so terribly depressed? [Why on earth should you feel depressed?] (*He kisses his wife on the cheek.*) Come, cheer up, darling! Let's live while there's life in us. Can't you send this depression packing, as Platonov says? Incidentally, talking of Platonov, why do you avoid him? He's not just anybody, you know. He's a most intelligent fellow, and far from boring. Have a good talk to him. A heart to heart talk. I'm sure he'll soon pull you out of this depression. And discuss things with mother more often, talk to Triletsky. (*Laughs.*) Yes, talk to them and don't treat them as if they were your inferiors. You don't know these people properly yet. I'd like you to know them better because they are people I'm very fond of. You, too, will like them when you know them better.

ANNA (*at the window*): Sergey! Sergey! Who's there? Tell Sergey I want him.

VOYNITSEV: What do you want me for?

ANNA: You're there? Come in for a moment.

VOYNITSEV: Coming. (*To* Sophia.) We'll be leaving if you haven't changed your mind by tomorrow. (*He goes into the house.*)

SOPHIA (*after a pause*): Why, this is almost a tragedy! Already I seem to be able not to think of my husband for days. I forget his presence. I pay no attention to what he is saying. I can no longer bear to be with him. [What am I to do? (*Thinks.*) It's awful!] Such a short time since our wedding, and already!... It's all the fault of that man—Platonov! I haven't the strength, [I haven't the willpower, there's nothing that could help me] to resist him. He pursues me from morning till night, keeps staring at me, doesn't give me a moment's peace with those understanding eyes of his. It's awful! And so stupid, too! The trouble is I can't answer for myself. He's only to take one step and anything may happen.

PLATONOV *comes out of the house.*

[SOPHIA: There he comes, looking for someone. Who is he looking for? I can see by the way he walks what he wants! How dishonourable of him not to give me a moment's peace!]

PLATONOV: It's hot! I oughtn't to have drunk so much... (*Catching sight of* Sophia.) You here, Sophia? All alone? (*He laughs.*)

SOPHIA: Yes.

PLATONOV: Avoiding us mortals?

SOPHIA: Why should I? I've nothing against them and they don't interfere with me.

PLATONOV: Oh? (*He sits down beside her.*) May I? (*Pause.*) But [if you're not avoiding people,] why then are you avoiding me? What have I done? Please, let me finish. I'm very glad to be able to have a talk to you at last. You avoid me, you keep out of my way, you don't look at me. What is it? A game, or are you serious?

SOPHIA: I'm sure it never occurred to me to avoid you. Whatever gave you that idea?

PLATONOV: At first you were quite pleased to see me, but now you avoid me. [You favoured me with your attentions. But now you don't want even to see me.] I come into one room, you go out into another. [I come into the garden, you rush out of the garden.] I start talking to you and all I get is a laconic 'no' or a resentful 'yes' [and off you go] . . . Our relationship has been transformed into a sort of misunderstanding. Is it my fault? [Do I disgust you?] (*He gets up.*) I'm quite sure I've done nothing to deserve such treatment. Have the goodness to put an end to this stupid situation which is too childish for words! [I shan't put up with it any longer!]

SOPHIA: I admit that—er—I do avoid you a little. Had I realized that you felt so badly about it, I'd have behaved differently.

PLATONOV: Avoid me? (*He sits down.*) So you admit it. But—why? What have I done?

SOPHIA: Please, don't shout. I mean, don't talk so loudly. [You're not reprimanding me, I hope.] I don't like people to shout at me. [It isn't you personally I am avoiding. I'm just trying to avoid talking to you.] You are, as far as I know, a decent man. Here everyone likes and respects you. Some, I believe, even have a very high opinion of you and are flattered to talk to you.

PLATONOV: I see. Well?

SOPHIA: At first I was only too glad to join your audience. But I was unlucky. [Yes, I certainly was unlucky.] You made me feel uncomfortable. Soon you became almost unbearable. I'm sorry I can't find a milder expression. Every day you kept telling me how you used to love me, how I used to love you, and so on. A student was in love with a young girl, and a young girl was in love with a student. It's too old and too ordinary a story to be worth talking about or for us to attach any importance to it. But that's not the point. The point is that when you talk to me about our past, you seem to talk in a way as though [you were asking for something, as though] you are hoping to get something now you failed to get then. Every day the tone of your voice is wearisomely the same. Every day I can't help feeling that you are hinting at some kind of obligations which our common past imposes upon us. It seems to me you're attaching a little too great an importance to our present relationship—that, to put it plainly, you are exaggerating our relationship of good friends. You look at me so strangely. You get excited, you shout, you grasp my hand, you follow me about. I get the feeling that you are spying on me. What is it all about? In fact, you're not giving me a moment's rest. Why all this supervision? What am I to you? Honestly I think you're just waiting for something to happen that would give you the chance you're hoping for. (*Pause.*)

PLATONOV: Is that all? (*Getting up.*) Thank you for your frankness. (*He walks towards the door.*)

SOPHIA: You're not angry with me, are you? (*She gets up.*) One moment, Platonov. Why take offence? I didn't want to—

PLATONOV (*stops in his tracks*): Oh, you! (*Pause.*) All this means, of course, that you're not tired of me, but that you're afraid, that you haven't the courage. Are you afraid, my dear Sophia? (*He walks up to her.*)

SOPHIA: [Drop it, Platonov.] You're quite wrong. I have never been afraid, and I've no intention of being afraid now.

PLATONOV: Where is your strength of character, where is that famous commonsense of yours if you regard every man who is just a little above the average as likely to be dangerous to your Sergey? I used to come here every day long before you arrived. I talked to you because I thought you were an intelligent and an understanding woman. What deep-seated depravity! However, I'm sorry. I get carried away. I have no right to say all this to you. I apologize for my stupid behaviour.

SOPHIA: You have no right to say such things! The fact that people listen to you doesn't give you the right to say anything that may enter your head. Go away!

PLATONOV (*bursts out laughing*): Followed about, are you? Pursued, grasped by the hand? Who's trying to take you away from your husband, you poor thing? Platonov is in love with you? The eccentric Platonov? What joy! What bliss! Why, such delightful dishes for that silly little vanity of yours no gourmet has ever tasted. It's too ridiculous for words! Such delights are not becoming to a well-educated young woman. (*He goes into the house.*)

SOPHIA: You're impertinent and rude, Platonov! You're mad! (*She follows him and stops at the front door.*) It's awful! Why did he say all this? He wanted to impress me, play on my feelings. I'm not going to put up with it! I'll go and tell him. (*She goes into the house.*)

OSIP *comes out from behind the pagoda.*

OSIP [(*entering*): Five good ones, six bad ones. Goodness only knows what they're doing. I'd better go and have a game of preference, or some other game of chance.] Hullo, Yakov. Is that—what's his name?—Vengerovich here?

YAKOV: Yes, he's here.

OSIP: Go and call him. Quietly. Tell him I want to discuss some important business with him.

YAKOV: All right. (*He goes into the house.*)

[OSIP (*pulls down a lantern, extinguishes it and puts it in his pocket*): In town last year I played cards at Daria Ivanovna's, the receiver of stolen goods who keeps an establishment with young ladies. The lowest stakes were three copeks. But the fines went up to two roubles. I won eight roubles. (*He pulls down another lantern.*) It's great fun in town.

VASILY (*comes in*): The lanterns are not hung for the likes of you. What are you pulling them down for?

OSIP: Fancy, I didn't see you at all! Hullo, old donkey, how are you? (*He walks up to him.*) How are you getting on? Oh, you horse, you—you swineherd you. (*He pulls off his cap.*) You're funny. Damn funny! Have you a drop of intelligence? (*He throws the cap on a tree.*) Slap my face for being a bad man!

VASILY: Let other fellows slap your face. I'm not going to do it.

OSIP: But will you kill me? If you have a grain of sense you'll kill me by yourself and not with a whole crowd of people. Spit in my face for being a bad man!

VASILY: I won't spit at you. Leave me alone, will you?

OSIP: So you won't spit at me? Afraid of me, are you? Go down on your knees before me! (*Pause.*) Well, kneel I say! Who am I talking to? A live man or a wall? (*Pause.*) Who am I talking to, I ask you.

VASILY (*going down on his knees*): You didn't ought to have done that.

OSIP: Ashamed to kneel? I like that! A gentleman in tails kneeling before a robber. Well? And now give three cheers, and as loud as you can . . . Well?

Enter VENGEROVICH SR.

VENGEROVICH SR. (*coming out of the house*): Who wants to see me?

OSIP (*takes off his hat with alacrity*): Me, sir.

[VASILY (*gets up, sits down on the bench and weeps*).]

VENGEROVICH SR.: What do you want?

OSIP: You were so good as to ask for me at the pub, sir. So here I am.

[VENGEROVICH SR.: Oh, yes, but—couldn't you choose a better place?

OSIP: For good men, sir, every place is good.]

VENGEROVICH SR.: I may want your services . . . Let's go [somewhere else. There—]to that bench. (*They go to a bench at the back of the stage.*) Stand a little further away, look as though you're not talking to me. That's right. Did the publican send you?

OSIP: Yes, sir.

VENGEROVICH SR.: He shouldn't have. It's not you I wanted, but—it can't be helped. [One can't do anything with you. I mean, one oughtn't to have anything to do with you. You're such a bad lot.

OSIP: Very. Worse than anyone in the world, sir.

VENGEROVICH SR.: Not so loud. The money I've been dishing out to you—you don't seem to appreciate it. Just as if my money was some useless thing—stones or something. You're so reckless. You steal. Turning away? Don't you like the truth? Unpalatable, is it?

OSIP: Well, sir, I don't mind truth but not your kind of truth. You did not ask me to come here to lecture me, did you, sir?

VENGEROVICH SR.: Not so loud.] Do you know—Platonov?

OSIP: The schoolmaster? Of course I know him.

VENGEROVICH SR.: Yes, the schoolmaster. The schoolmaster who teaches abuse and nothing else. How much will you take to cripple him?

OSIP: How do you mean—cripple him?

VENGEROVICH SR.: I mean cripple, not kill. One shouldn't kill people. [Why kill them? Murder is something that . . .] Cripple him, that is, give him such a beating that he'll remember it all his life.

OSIP: Yes, I can do that.

VENGEROVICH SR.: Break some bones, or disfigure his face.

[How much?] Shhh! Someone's coming. Let's go further away.

> *They go towards the back of the stage.* PLATONOV *and* MARY *come out of the house.*

PLATONOV (*laughing*): What? What did you say? (*He bursts out laughing.*) I'm sorry, I didn't quite catch that.

MARY: Didn't you? Well, I can repeat it. I can express myself even more bluntly. I take it you won't be offended, of course. You're so used to rudeness of every sort that you'll hardly be surprised at my words.

PLATONOV: Come on, come on, say it, beautiful!

MARY: I am not beautiful. Anyone who thinks I'm beautiful has no taste. Tell me frankly. I'm not beautiful, am I? What do you think?

PLATONOV: I'll tell you later. It's your turn to speak.

MARY: Very well, listen. You are either an extraordinary sort of person or—a scoundrel, either one or the other.

PLATONOV (*laughs at the top of his voice*).

MARY: You laugh? Well, yes, it is rather funny. (*She laughs.*)

PLATONOV (*laughs*): She said it. What a silly little darling! How do you like that! (*He puts his arm around her waist.*)

MARY (*sits down*): Please, don't . . .

PLATONOV: She, too, is a person of some consequence! Philosophizes, studies chemistry, and delivers herself of all sorts of aphorisms. What's one to do with her? The silly little thing! (*He kisses her.*) You pretty, bizarre little rogue.

MARY: Please . . . What's all this? I—I didn't say . . . (*She gets up and sits down again.*) Why do you kiss me? I have done nothing to . . .

PLATONOV: She said and surprised me. Let's say something striking, she said to herself, and astonish him. Let him see what a clever girl I am! (*He kisses her.*) Look at her! She doesn't know what to do. She looks embarrassed. Stares stupidly. Oh dear, oh dear.

MARY: Are you—are you in love with me? Are you?

PLATONOV (*in a squeaky voice*): And do you love me?

MARY: If—if—then—yes. (*She weeps.*) You do love me, don't you, or you wouldn't have behaved like that. Do you love me?

PLATONOV: Not a bit, my sweet. I don't love silly little girls, sinner that I am. I love one silly girl, but even her I love because I've nothing else to do. Oh, she's turned pale. Her eyes flash. 'I'll show you. I'll show you! I won't be trifled with.'

MARY (*rising*): Are you laughing at me? (*Pause.*)

PLATONOV: If I'm not careful she'll slap my face.

MARY: I am proud. I'm not going to soil my hands. I've told you, my dear sir, that you are either an extraordinary person or a scoundrel, and now I'm telling you that you're an extraordinary scoundrel. I despise you! (*She goes away towards the house.*) I'm not going to cry now. I'm glad that at last I have found out exactly the sort of person you are.

Enter TRILETSKY *in a top hat.*

TRILETSKY: The cranes are crying . . . Where have they come from? (*He looks up at the sky.*) So early.

MARY: If you have any respect for me at all, doctor, have nothing to do with this man! (*She points to* Platonov.)

TRILETSKY (*laughing*): Good Lord, my dear girl, this is one of my most respected relatives.

MARY: And friend?

TRILETSKY: And friend.

MARY: I do not envy you. And I don't think I envy him, either. You're a kind man, but—this jocular tone . . . Sometimes I feel sick of your jokes. I'm sorry, I meant no offence, but—I've been insulted and you're joking. (*Cries.*) I've been insulted . . . Still, I oughtn't to cry. I am proud. Go on knowing this man, love him, show respect for his intellect, fear him . . . You all seem to think he's a second Hamlet. Well, admire him! I don't

care. I don't want anything from you. Joke as much as you like with this—scoundrel! (*She goes into the house.*)
TRILETSKY (*after a pause*): Satisfied, old man?
PLATONOV: I haven't eaten anything so how can I be satisfied?
TRILETSKY: It's high time, my dear fellow, you left her alone. You really ought to be ashamed of yourself, an intelligent man like you, a man of such great abilities, carrying on goodness only knows how. Is it any wonder you've been called a scoundrel? (*Pause.*) You can't really expect me to tear myself in two: one half to respect you and the other to have serious intentions towards a girl who has called you a scoundrel.
PLATONOV: Don't respect me and you won't have to tear yourself in two.
TRILETSKY: But I can't help respecting you. You don't know what you're saying.
PLATONOV: Well, in that case, there's only one thing left: don't have any serious intentions towards her. I don't understand you, Nicholas. What have you, an intelligent man, found in a silly girl like that?
TRILETSKY: Well, Anna often accuses me of being no gentleman and points to you as a model gentleman. But in my opinion this accusation can be made against you, [the model,] also. All of them, and especially you, are shouting from the housetops that I'm in love with her, are laughing at me, mocking me, suspecting all sorts of things, spying on me.
PLATONOV: Express yourself more clearly—do!
TRILETSKY: I'm expressing myself quite clearly, I think. At the same time, you have the effrontery to call her in my presence a little fool and worthless creature. No, you're not a gentleman. Gentlemen know that people who're in love have a certain pride. She's no fool, my dear chap, she's no fool. She's just your scapegoat. That's what she is. There are moments, my dear friend, when one wants to hate someone, to sink one's teeth into someone, vent one's spite on someone, so why not

try it on her? She'll do. She's weak, defenceless, gazes at you with such foolishly trustful eyes. I understand it all perfectly well... (*Getting up.*) [Come, let's have a drink.

OSIP (*to* Vengerovich Sr.): If you don't pay me the rest after it's done, I shall steal a hundred times more from you. You can be sure of that.

VENGEROVICH SR. (*to* Osip): Not so loud. When you're beating him, don't forget to say, 'This is from the grateful publican.' Shhhh. Go now. (*He goes towards the house.*)

OSIP *goes out.*]

TRILETSKY: I say, Mr. Vengerovich. (*To* Vengerovich Sr.) You're not ill, by any chance, are you?

VENGEROVICH SR.: Don't worry, I'm quite all right.

TRILETSKY: What a pity. You see, I want money badly just now. You believe me, don't you? I need it desperately, as they say.

VENGEROVICH SR.: Which, doctor, is the same as saying that you want patients desperately. Am I right? (*He laughs.*)

TRILETSKY: Very funny! [A bit heavy, but to the point.] Ha, ha, ha, and again ha, ha, ha! Why don't you laugh, Platonov? Come on, lend me some, there's a good fellow.

VENGEROVICH SR.: But you owe me a lot as it is, doctor.

TRILETSKY: Why mention it? Who doesn't know it? Anyway, how much do I owe you?

VENGEROVICH SR.: About—well—two hundred and forty-five roubles, I think.

TRILETSKY: Give, O great man. Do me a favour and one day I'll do you a favour, too. Be kind, generous, and brave! [The bravest Jew is he who gives a loan without an I.O.U. Be the most brave Jew!

VENGEROVICH SR.: Well, yes. A Jew. Always Jews, Jews. I assure you, gentlemen, that I never saw a Russian who would give you money without an I.O.U. and nowhere is the practice so widespread of giving money without I.O.U.'s as among the dishonest Jews. May I drop dead on this spot if I'm telling a lie. (*Sighs.*) There are many, many things, young man, you could learn to your advantage from us Jews, and especially from us elderly Jews. Yes, many, many things. (*He takes out his wallet.*) One lends you money willingly and with pleasure and you—you like to laugh at us, to make fun of us. This isn't nice, gentlemen. I'm an old man, I have children. Think me a scoundrel if you like, but treat me as a human being. Isn't that why you studied at the university?

TRILETSKY: You speak well, my dear fellow.

VENGEROVICH SR.: It's not nice, gentlemen. Not nice at all. One might think that there was no difference whatever between men of good education like you, and my clerks, and no one has given you permission to be familiar with me. How much do you want? Yes, it's very bad, young man.] How much do you want?

TRILETSKY: As much as you'll give me. (*Pause.*)

VENGEROVICH SR.: I'll give you—I can give you—fifty roubles. (*He gives him the money.*)

TRILETSKY: Marvellous! (*Taking the money.*) You're great!

VENGEROVICH SR.: You're wearing my hat, doctor.

TRILETSKY: Yours? Well . . . (*Taking off hat.*) Take it! [Why don't you have it cleaned? It's not expensive. What do you call a top hat in Jewish?

VENGEROVICH SR.: Call it what you like. (*Puts on his hat.*)

TRILETSKY: A top hat suits you. A baron, a real baron! Why don't you buy yourself a barony?

VENGEROVICH SR.: I don't know what you're talking about. Leave me alone, will you?

TRILETSKY: You're a great man. Why is it that people don't want to understand you?]

VENGEROVICH SR.: Why don't you leave me alone? (*He goes into the house.*)

PLATONOV: Why did you take that money from him?

TRILETSKY: Why? Just because. (*He sits down.*)

PLATONOV: What do you mean—just because?

TRILETSKY: I took it, and that's all. Why? You're not sorry for him, are you?

PLATONOV: That's not the point, old man.

TRILETSKY: What, then, is the point?

PLATONOV: Don't you know?

TRILETSKY: I don't know.

PLATONOV: You're a liar. You know very well. (*Pause.*) [My heart would have been fired with a great love for you, my dear fellow, if you'd agree to live according to some rules, however light, just for one week, even for one day. For men like you rules are as necessary as daily bread. (*Pause.*)]

TRILETSKY: I don't know anything. It isn't your business or mine to change human nature. It is not men like us who can do that. [I knew that even as far back as when you and I were getting the lowest marks in Latin. Don't let us, therefore, waste our time on idle talk. May our tongues cleave to our palates!] (*Pause.*) The other day I was examining the portraits of our 'contemporary public figures' [at the house of one of my lady friends] and reading their biographies. And what do you think, my dear chap? You and I are not among them. [No, sir. Couldn't find either you or myself, however much I tried. *Lasciate*, my dear friend, *ogni speranza*, as the Italians say. I couldn't find either you or myself among our 'contemporary public figures'] and—can you imagine it?—I'm perfectly happy. Now, Sophia is different. She is not happy.

PLATONOV: What has Sophia to do with it?

TRILETSKY: She feels hurt not to be among our 'contemporary public figures'. She imagines she has only to move her little finger and the whole world will gape in astonishment at her and mankind will fling up its cap for sheer joy. She imagines—well —I'm afraid you won't find so much fatuous nonsense in any of our clever modern novels as you'll find in her. But, as a matter of fact, she isn't worth a brass farthing. Ice! Stone! A statue! I always feel like going up and chipping a bit of plaster of Paris off her nose. At the slightest thing—at once, hysterics, screams, sighs. Not an ounce of strength in her . . . A clever doll . . . Looks on me with contempt, thinks I'm just a blot on the landscape. But in what way is her darling Sergey better than you or me? Is it because he drinks no vodka, thinks elevated thoughts, and unblushingly describes himself as the man of the future? However, judge not lest ye be judged. (*Getting up.*) Come, let's have a drink.

PLATONOV: I'm not going. It's too close in there.

TRILETSKY: I'll go myself. (*Stretching himself.*) [Incidentally, what does that monogram 'S.V.' mean? Sophia Voynitsev, or Sergey Voynitsev? To whom did our philologist wish to pay his respects by these letters: his wife or himself?

PLATONOV: It seems to me that these letters must mean 'Salute to Vengerovich'. It's his money we are making merry on.

TRILETSKY: To be sure.] I say, what's the matter with Anna today? Laughs, moans, kisses everyone. Just as if she were in love.

PLATONOV: Who can she fall in love with here? With herself? Don't believe her laughter. It's impossible to believe the laughter of an intelligent woman who never cries. She laughs when she wants to cry. And our Anna doesn't want to cry, she wants to shoot herself. You can see it in her eyes.

TRILETSKY: Women never shoot themselves, they take poison. [But don't let's start an argument! When I'm arguing I talk the most utter rot.] Our general's lady is a nice woman. I must say I get all sorts of lascivious thoughts when I look at a woman, but she's the only woman from whom my carnal desires rebound like peas off a wall. The only one. When I look at her matter-of-fact face I begin to believe in platonic love. Coming?

PLATONOV: No.

TRILETSKY: Ah well, I'll go and have a drink with the priest. (*He goes and bumps into* Glagolyev Jr. *in the door*.) Sorry, your lordship, self-made count. Here's three roubles for you! (*He thrusts into his hand three roubles and goes off*.)

GLAGOLYEV JR.: What a strange fellow! For no reason at all—'Here's three roubles for you!' (*He shouts*.) I can give you three roubles myself! What an idiot! (*To* Platonov.) I'm quite amazed by his stupidity. (*He laughs*.) Horribly stupid!

PLATONOV: I believe you're very fond of dancing. Why, then, don't you dance?

GLAGOLYEV JR.: Dance? Here? With whom, may I ask? (*He sits down beside* Platonov.)

PLATONOV: No one to dance with?

GLAGOLYEV JR.: What a rabble! What specimens! The airs they give themselves! Such ugly faces, such crooked noses! And the women? (*Laughing loudly*.) Good Lord! In such company I invariably prefer the refreshment bar to dancing. (*Pause*.) How stale the air is in Russia! So damp, so close. I can't bear Russia. The ignorance, the stench—horrible! It's quite different abroad. Have you ever been to Paris?

PLATONOV: Afraid I haven't.

GLAGOLYEV JR.: Pity. Still I suppose you'll get there one day. Let me know when you'll be going there. I'll reveal all the mysteries of Paris to you. I'll give you three hundred letters of introduction and I'll put three hundred of the most *chic* French cocottes at your disposal.

PLATONOV: Thank you, I'm quite satisfied as it is. Tell me, is it true that your father wants to buy the estate?

GLAGOLYEV JR.: I'm sure I don't know. I'm afraid I'm not interested in business. Did you notice the attentions *mon père* is paying to your general's widow. (*Laughs at the top of his voice*.) There's another specimen for you. The old badger wants to get married! The silly fool! I must say your general's widow is *charmante*. Not at all bad. (*Pause*.) She's a real darling, in fact. Those curves! Dear me! (*Slaps* Platonov *on the shoulder*.) You are a lucky beggar! Does she wear corsets? Does she lace herself up tightly?

PLATONOV: I don't know. I'm not there when she's dressing.

GLAGOLYEV JR.: But I was told—Aren't you her . . .

PLATONOV: Count, you're an idiot!

GLAGOLYEV JR.: Oh, I was only joking. Why be angry? What an extraordinary fellow you are, to be sure! (*In a low voice.*) And is it true what they say about her—I'm afraid it's rather an impertinent question, but as it's just between ourselves I think—er—Is it true that she loves money? I mean, terribly?

PLATONOV: Why don't you ask her yourself? I don't know.

GLAGOLYEV JR.: Ask her myself? (*He laughs loudly.*) What an idea! What are you saying, Platonov?

PLATONOV (*sits down on another bench*): What a wonderful genius you have for boring people!

GLAGOLYEV JR. (*laughs loudly*): What if I were to ask her myself? Why shouldn't I ask her?

PLATONOV: Naturally. (*Aside.*) You ask her and she'll slap your silly face for you. (*To* Glagolyev Jr.) Ask her by all means.

GLAGOLYEV JR. (*jumping up*): By Jove! It's a great idea! Hell and damnation! I will ask her, Platonov, and on my word of honour she is mine! I have such a presentiment! I shall ask her at once! I bet you she's mine! (*Runs towards the house and comes face to face with* Anna *and* Triletsky.) *Mille pardons, madame.* (*He scrapes his feet and goes out.*)

PLATONOV *resumes his old seat.*

TRILETSKY (*on the front steps*): There he sits, our great sage and philosopher. Always on the look out. Waiting impatiently for his prey: whom to regale with a lecture before bedtime.

ANNA: I'm afraid Michael is not biting.

TRILETSKY: That's bad. Not biting today for some reason. Poor old moralist! I'm sorry for you, Platonov. I'm afraid I'm drunk and the priest is waiting for me. Good-bye. (*Goes out.*)

ANNA (*walking up to* Platonov): What are you sitting here for?

PLATONOV: It's close indoors and this lovely sky is better than the ceiling whitewashed by your village women.

ANNA (*sitting down*): What lovely weather! Pure, cool air, a starry sky, and a moon. What a pity ladies are not supposed to sleep in the open. When I was a little girl, I always slept in the garden in summer. (*Pause.*) Is that a new tie you're wearing?

PLATONOV: Yes. (*Pause.*)

ANNA: I'm in a peculiar mood today. Everything seems to please me. I feel like having a good time. Do say something, Platonov. Why are you silent? I came here to hear you talk. What a horrid fellow you are!

PLATONOV: What do you want me to tell you?

ANNA: Tell me something new, something nice, something spicy. You're so clever today, so handsome. I do believe I'm in love with you more than ever today. You're such a darling this evening. On your best behaviour, too.

PLATONOV: You, too, are very beautiful today, but then, you're always beautiful.

ANNA: Are we friends, Platonov?

PLATONOV: I suppose so. Yes, I suppose we are friends. What else would you call friendship?

ANNA: Friends at any rate, aren't we?

PLATONOV: Yes, I think we're great friends. I'm used to you and I'm greatly attached to you. It would take a lot of time to make me want to do without your company.

ANNA: Great friends?

PLATONOV: Why all these leading questions? Friends, friends! Just like an old maid.

ANNA: Very well, we are friends. But do you realize that with a man and a woman there's only one step from friendship to love? (*She laughs.*)

PLATONOV: I see! (*He laughs.*) Why are you saying this? You and I will never go too far.

ANNA: Love—going too far. Aren't they one and the same thing? Your wife cannot hear you. I'm sorry, but why shouldn't we go too far? Aren't we human beings? Love's an excellent thing. Why blush for it?

PLATONOV (*looking closely at her*): I can see that you are either joking charmingly or else you want to—come to some arrangement. Come, let's waltz.

ANNA: You can't dance. (*Pause.*) I must have a real talk to you. It's high time . . . (*She looks round.*) Try and listen to me for a moment—and, please, no philosophizing.

PLATONOV: Let's go inside and dance, Anna.

ANNA: Let's sit down a little further off. Come here. (*She sits down on another bench.*) The trouble is, I don't know how to begin. You're such a big, awkward, deceptive fellow . . .

PLATONOV: Don't you think I'd better begin, my dear Anna?

ANNA: But you talk a lot of nonsense, Platonov, when you start. Look at him! He's embarrassed. Like hell he is! (*She slaps Platonov on the shoulder.*) You're a great joker, Michael. All right, talk. Only make it brief.

PLATONOV: I shall be brief. What I want to say to you is this: whatever for? (*Pause.*) It's not worth it, Anna. Take my word for it.

ANNA: Why not? Please, listen. You don't understand me. If you were free, I'd marry you without giving it a second thought. I'd sacrifice my title for you. But now . . . Well? Is silence a sign of consent? Is it? (*Pause.*) Listen, Platonov, in a case like this, it's not decent to remain silent.

PLATONOV (*jumping up*): Let's forget this conversation, Anna. For God's sake, let's behave as though it had never taken place! Never!

ANNA (*shrugs*): What a strange man you are! Why not?

PLATONOV: Because I respect you. I respect this feeling of mine for you so much that I'd find it easier to sink through the ground than to get rid of it. My dear friend, I do as I like. I depend on no one. I don't mind having a nice time and I'm not against having affairs with women. I'm not even against having some high-minded affair, but—to have some sordid little affair with you, to make you the object of my idle thoughts, a clever, beautiful, free woman like you—no! [That is too much. Better drive me away to the other end of the world!] To spend a stupid month or two together and then to part and blush at the memory of it?

ANNA: We're talking about love.

PLATONOV: But don't I love you? I love you—good, intelligent, compassionate woman. I love you desperately, madly. I'm ready to lay down my life for you if you so wish. I love you as a woman, as a human being. Must every kind of love be misrepresented as only a certain kind of love? My love is a thousand times more precious to me than the one you've so suddenly got into your head!

ANNA (*getting up*): Go and have a good sleep, my dear. We will continue our talk afterwards.

PLATONOV: Let's forget this conversation. (*He kisses her hand.*) Let's be friends. Don't let's play the fool with one another. We deserve something better. And besides, I am, you know, just—a little bit married. [Let's drop this conversation. Let it all be as it was before.]

ANNA: Go, my dear, go! Married... But you love me, don't you? Why, then, talk about your wife? Go! We'll talk about it later. In an hour or two. Now you seem to be suffering from an attack of prevarication.

PLATONOV: I should never dream of lying to you. (*He whispers in her ear.*) If I knew how to lie to you, my darling, I'd have been your lover long ago.

ANNA (*sharply*): Go!

PLATONOV: Nonsense, you're not angry with me at all. You're just pretending. (*He goes into the house.*)

ANNA: What an extraordinary man! (*She sits down.*) Doesn't he realize what he is saying. [Misrepresent every kind of love as a certain kind of love! What nonsense! Like the love of a novelist for a lady novelist. (*Pause.*) Insufferable man! We'll waste our time chattering till doomsday like this, my dear friend.] If I can't take you fairly, I shall take you by force. This very night! [It's time for both of us to get out of this absurd state of suspense. I'm fed up. I'll take you by force.] Who is this coming? Glagolyev—looking for me.

GLAGOLYEV SR. *enters.*

GLAGOLYEV SR.: I'm bored. These people say things I've heard years ago. [They think what I thought as a child. It's all] old stuff, nothing new. I'll have a talk to her and leave.

ANNA: What are you muttering about, my dear Porfiry? May I know?

GLAGOLYEV SR.: You're here? (*He goes up to her.*) I'm cursing myself for being unwanted here.

ANNA: Because you're not like us? People learn to live with cockroaches, why don't you learn to live with our sort of people? Sit down. Let's have a talk.

GLAGOLYEV SR. (*sits down beside her*): I was looking for you, my dear Anna. There's something I'd like to discuss with you.

ANNA: Well, let's discuss it.

GLAGOLYEV SR.: Yes, I'd like to have a talk with you. I'd like to know your answer to my—letter.

ANNA: What do you want with me, my dear Porfiry?

GLAGOLYEV SR.: Well, you see, I'm quite willing to—er—give up any claims to—er—any conjugal rights. I'm no longer interested in those rights. But I want a friend, an intelligent mistress for my household. I own a paradise, but there are no—angels in it.

ANNA [(*aside*): Every word he utters is like a lump of sugar. (*To him.*)] I often ask myself what I'd do in paradise if I ever got there, for, you see, I'm a human being and not an angel.

GLAGOLYEV SR.: How can you possibly know what you're going to do in paradise if you don't know what you're going to do tomorrow. A good woman will find something to do everywhere —on earth as well as in heaven.

ANNA: All this is excellent, but will my life in your house be worth what I shall be getting for it? You must admit the whole thing is a little odd. I'm sorry but it's your proposal that seems very odd to me. What do you want to marry for? What do you want a friend in a petticoat for? It's no business of mine, of course, but as we've gone this far, I'd better finish. Had I been your age and had I had your money, your intelligence, and your sense of justice, I'd look for nothing else in this world except the general good. To put it more plainly, I'd have looked for no further reward than the love of my neighbours.

GLAGOLYEV SR.: I'm afraid I'm not the man to fight for the happiness of people. To do that, one has to possess an iron will and the right sort of ability, and it's just those things that God did not bestow on me. I was born to love great deeds and to perform lots of little and worthless ones. Only to love! Come to me, please.

ANNA: No, sir. Don't say another word about it. Don't attach any vital importance to my refusal. Vanity, my friend! If we could possess all the things we love, we should have no room left for —our possessions. Which means that it's not always silly or impolite to refuse. (*She bursts out laughing.*) There's a piece of philosophy for you as a tailpiece. What's that noise? Do you hear? I bet it's Platonov starting a row. What a character!

MARY *and* TRILETSKY *enter*.

MARY (*entering*): I can't bear such insults any more. (*She cries.*) I can't! Only persons with no sense of decency can remain silent when they see this sort of thing.

TRILETSKY: I agree, I agree. But what have I got to do with it? What have I got to do with it? You don't expect me to knock him on the head, do you?

MARY: I do, if there's no other way. Go away from me. I, a woman, would not have remained silent if you'd been insulted so basely, so shamelessly and so underservedly in front of me.

TRILETSKY: But I did protest. Talk sense. How am I to blame?

MARY: You're a coward, that's what you are. Go away to your revolting refreshment bar. Goodbye. Don't bother to come to see me again. We don't need one another. Good-bye.

TRILETSKY: All right. Good-bye, if you insist. I'm sick and tired of it all. I've had enough. Tears, tears! Good Lord, my head's spinning. *Coenurus cerebralis.* Oh dear! (*Waves and goes out.*)

MARY: *Coenurus cerebralis.* (*She is about to go.*) He insulted me. Why? What did I do?

ANNA (*going up to her*): My dear Mary, I don't want to stop you. I'd go myself, if I were in your place. (*She kisses her.*) Don't cry, my dear. Most women were created to put up with all sorts of disgusting things from men.

MARY: But not me. I shall get him sacked. He won't be a teacher here any more. He has no right to be a teacher. Tomorrow I'll go to the inspector of elementary schools ...

ANNA: Now, now, my dear. I'll come and see you in a day or two and we shall discuss what to do with Platonov together. Please, calm yourself now. Stop crying. You will get satisfaction. And, please, my dear, don't be angry with Triletsky. He didn't stand up for you because he's too kindhearted and soft and people like that are not capable of standing up for anybody. What did he do to you?

MARY: He kissed me in front of everyone, he called me a fool and pushed me on to a table. Don't imagine that I'm going to let him get away with it. He's either a madman or ... I'll show him. (*She goes out.*)

ANNA (*after her*): Good-bye. I'll be seeing you soon. (*To* Yakov.) Yakov, get Miss Grekov's carriage for her. Oh, Platonov, Platonov! He'll get himself into serious trouble one day with his brawling.

GLAGOLYEV SR.: What a nice girl! Our most excellent Platonov doesn't seem to like her very much. Treats her very badly.

ANNA: For no reason in the world. Today he insults her and tomorrow he apologizes. That's the old aristocrat in him.

Enter GLAGOLYEV JR.

GLAGOLYEV JR. (*aside*): With her! Again with her! Damn it all, this is going a bit too far! (*He glares at his father.*)

GLAGOLYEV SR. (*after a pause*): What do you want?

GLAGOLYEV JR.: You're sitting here, and they're looking for you there. You'd better go. They're calling you.

GLAGOLYEV SR.: Who's calling me?

GLAGOLYEV JR.: People.

GLAGOLYEV SR.: I know it's people . . . (*He gets up.*) Say what you like, but I will not give you up, my dear Anna. Perhaps you'll talk differently when you've understood me. I shall be seeing you. (*He goes into the house.*)

GLAGOLYEV JR. (*sits down beside* Anna): The old badger! The donkey! No one's calling him. I told him a lie.

ANNA: When you grow a little more intelligent you'll be very sorry for treating your father like that.

GLAGOLYEV JR.: You must be joking. This is what I've come here for. A couple of words. Yes or no?

ANNA: What do you mean?

GLAGOLYEV JR. (*laughing*): As if you didn't know. Yes or no?

ANNA: I simply don't know what you're talking about!

GLAGOLYEV JR.: You will in a moment. With the aid of gold everything is understood. If it's 'yes' then will you, generalissimo of my heart, slip your hand in my pocket and pull out my wallet with dear Papa's money. (*He holds up his side pocket.*)

ANNA: It's frank, at any rate. Why, don't you know that clever people get their faces slapped for saying such things?

GLAGOLYEV JR.: To have your face slapped by an attractive woman must be quite an attractive proposition. First she slaps your face and a little later she says 'yes'.

ANNA (*standing up*): Take your hat and clear out of here at once.

GLAGOLYEV JR. (*getting up*): Where?

ANNA: Wherever you like. Get out and don't you ever dare show your face here again.

GLAGOLYEV JR.: Good heavens, why get so angry? I shan't go.

ANNA: In that case, I'll have you thrown out.

GLAGOLYEV JR.: You *are* angry. I didn't say anything in particular. What did I say? There's no need to be angry. (*He follows her into the house.*)

PLATONOV *and* SOPHIA *come out of the house.*

PLATONOV: At school I'm still working as an ordinary teacher, a job for which I am not exactly cut out. That's all that's happened since we last met. (*They sit down.*) I can see iniquity all round. I can see it defiling the earth, swallowing up my brothers in Christ and my countrymen, but I sit about without doing anything, arms folded, as if I had just finished some arduous task. I sit, I look on, I eat, I am silent. I'm twenty-seven, but when I'm thirty I shall be just the same as I am now. I anticipate no change. As the years roll by, I can see myself growing fat, dull, and completely indifferent to everything except the lusts of the flesh, and then—death. A life completely ruined! My hair stands on end when I think of this kind of death. How am I to rise, Sophy? (*Pause.*) You are silent. You don't know. And indeed, how are you to know? I'm not sorry for myself, Sophy. To hell with me! But what has happened to you? Where is your pure soul, your sincerity, your sense of justice? Where is your courage? What's happened to your health? Where did you leave it? My dear Sophy, to spend whole years doing nothing, to make other hands do your work for you, to gaze at the suffering of other people and at the same time to be able to look people straight in the face—why, this is depravity! (Sophia *gets up, but* Platonov *makes her sit down.*) This is my last word. So, please, wait. What has made you into such a posturing, idle, phrasemongering woman? Who taught you to lie? How different you were before! Please, let me finish. How wonderful you were, how great. Darling Sophy, perhaps you can still rise. Perhaps it's not too late. Think! Gather up your strength and raise yourself, for God's sake! (*He seizes her by the hand.*) My dear, tell me frankly, in the name of our common past, what made you marry that man? How could such a marriage have appealed to you?

SOPHIA: He's an excellent man.

PLATONOV: Don't say things you don't believe in.

SOPHIA (*getting up*): He's my husband and I'll thank you not to . . .

PLATONOV: Let him be anything he likes, but I shall speak the truth. Sit down! (*He makes her resume her seat.*) Why didn't you choose for your husband a man who works hard, a man who has suffered for his beliefs? Why didn't you take *anyone* for your husband, and not this pygmy who's up to his neck in debt and hasn't done a stroke of work all his life.

SOPHIA: Stop it! Don't shout! There's someone coming.

Several guests are passing by.

PLATONOV: To hell with them! Let them all hear. (*He lowers his voice.*) I'm sorry I was too harsh. But, you see, I loved you. I loved you more than anything in the world, and that's why you're still dear to me even now. I loved this hair, these hands, this face so much. Why do you powder your face, Sophia? Don't do it. Oh dear, if you'd come across another man you'd have risen soon enough, but here you'll only sink deeper and deeper into the mire. Poor thing! . . . If I had the strength I should have torn you up by the roots from this swamp and myself as well. (*Pause.*) Life! Why don't we live as we should?

SOPHIA (*gets up and covers her face with her hands*): Leave me alone! (*A noise can be heard in the house.*) Go away! (*She walks towards the house.*)

PLATONOV (*following her*): Take your hands away from your face. So! You won't go abroad, will you? Let's be friends, Sophy. You won't go away and we shall have another talk, shan't we? Yes? (*The noise in the house gets louder and people can be heard running down the stairs.*)

SOPHIA: Yes.

PLATONOV: Let's be friends, my dear. Why should we be enemies? Please, a few more words.

> VOYNITSEV, *followed by a number of guests, comes running out of the house.*

VOYNITSEV: Ah, there they are, the people we are looking for. Come, let's go and set off the fireworks. (*Shouts.*) Yakov! Off to the river! (*To* Sophia.) Have you changed your mind, Sophy?

PLATONOV: She's not going. She's staying here.

VOYNITSEV: She is? Ah, well, in that case—hurrah! Your hand, Michael. (*Presses* Platonov's *hand.*) I always used to fall under the spell of your eloquence myself. Come, let's go and set off the fireworks. (*He goes off with the other guests into the garden.*)

PLATONOV (*after a pause*): Yes, my dear Sophy, that's how it is! Well?

VOYNITSEV (*off stage*): Mother, where are you? Platonov! (*Pause.*)

PLATONOV: Hell, I suppose I'd better go. (*Shouts.*) Sergey, wait! Don't set them off without me! (*Addressing a servant.*) Send Yakov to me for the balloon, my good man. (*He runs off into the garden.*)

ANNA (*running out of the house*): Wait, Sergey, wait! Not everyone's here yet. Go on firing the cannon. (*To* Sophia.) Come along, Sophia. Why are you looking so sad?

PLATONOV (*off stage*): This way, your ladyship. We'll strike up the old song without starting a new one.

ANNA: Coming! (*She runs off.*)
PLATONOV (*off stage*): Who's coming in the boat with me? Won't you come for a sail on the river with me, Sophia?
SOPHIA: Shall I?
[TRILETSKY (*comes in*): Hey, where are you? (*Sings.*) I'm coming, I'm coming! (*He stares at* Sophia.)
SOPHIA: What do you want?
TRILETSKY: Nothing, nothing at all.
SOPHIA: Why don't you go away then? I'm not in the mood for talking or listening today.
TRILETSKY: I know, I know. (*Pause.*) For some reason I'd like terribly to run a finger over your forehead to see what it's made of. I'd awfully like to know. Not to offend you, you understand, but just—to satisfy myself.
SOPHIA: Buffoon! (*She turns away.*) You're not a comic, you're a buffoon! A clown.
TRILETSKY: Yes. A buffoon. Didn't you know I was getting my board and lodgings from her ladyship for being her jester? And pocket money, too. When they tire of me, they'll kick me out of here in disgrace. It's true what I'm saying, isn't it. However, I'm not the only one who says it. You said it too at dinner at Glagolyev's, didn't you?
SOPHIA: I did, I did. I'm very glad you've been told about it. Now you know that I can differentiate between buffoons and men with a real sense of humour. Had you been an actor, you'd be the favourite of the gallery, but the stalls would boo you. I am booing you.
TRILETSKY: Your joke is quite supernaturally successful. Very nice. Let me bid you good-bye. (*He bows.*) Till we meet again in more pleasant circumstances, I hope. I'd have liked to have another talk with you, but I'm—too timid. I'm struck dumb. (*He goes off into the garden.*)
SOPHIA (*stamping her foot*): The horrible man! He doesn't know what I really think of him. Emptyheaded little fool!]

PLATONOV (*off stage*): Who's coming on the river with me?
SOPHIA: Well, what must be, must be. (*She shouts.*) I'm coming!
(*She runs off.*)

GLAGOLYEV SR. *and* GLAGOLYEV JR. *come out of the house.*

GLAGOLYEV SR.: You're lying. You're lying, you dirty-minded whipper-snapper!
GLAGOLYEV JR.: Don't talk such nonsense! Why on earth should I lie? Ask her yourself if you don't believe me. As soon as you'd gone, I whispered a few words in her ear on this very bench, put my arm round her and gave her a smacking big kiss right on the mouth. First she asked for three thousand, but after a little haggling she agreed to take one thousand. So let me have one thousand roubles, please.
GLAGOLYEV SR.: Cyril, a woman's honour is at stake. Don't besmirch it. It's sacred. I won't hear another word.
GLAGOLYEV JR.: I swear by my honour. Don't you believe me? [I swear by all the saints.] Come, give me the thousand roubles. I shall take them to her at once . . .
GLAGOLYEV SR.: This is awful. You're lying! She must have pulled your leg. A fool like you.
GLAGOLYEV JR.: But I'm telling you, I embraced her. What's so surprising about that? All women are like that now. Don't you believe in their innocence. I know them. And you were thinking of getting married! (*He bursts out laughing.*)
GLAGOLYEV SR.: For God's sake, Cyril, don't you know the meaning of slander?
GLAGOLYEV JR.: Give me one thousand roubles. I'll give them to her in your presence. I tell you I put my arm round her on this very bench, kissed her, haggled with her. I swear it's true. What more do you want? Don't you realize that I made you go into the house so that I could agree about a price with her? He doesn't believe I know how to conquer women. Offer her two thousand and she's yours. I know women, my dear sir.

GLAGOLYEV SR. (*pulls his wallet out of his pocket and throws it down on the ground*): Take it.

GLAGOLYEV JR. (*picks up the wallet and counts the money*).

VOYNITSEV (*off stage*): I'm starting. Mother, fire! Triletsky, climb up on the pagoda! Who has stepped on to the box? You?

TRILETSKY (*off stage*): I am climbing up, damn it. (*He laughs at the top of his voice.*) Who's that? Someone's knocked down Bugrov. I've stepped on Bugrov's head. Where are the matches?

GLAGOLYEV JR. (*aside*): I'm revenged. (*He shouts.*) Hurrah! Hurrah! (*He runs off.*)

TRILETSKY (*off stage*): Who's shouting there? Punch him on the nose!

VOYNITSEV (*off stage*): Shall we start?

GLAGOLYEV SR. (*clutching his head*): Good Lord! Depravity! Corruption! I worshipped her. Forgive her, O Lord. (*He sits down on the bench and buries his face in his hands.*)

VOYNITSEV (*off stage*): Who's taken the string? Mother, aren't you ashamed of yourself? Where is the string? It was lying here a minute ago.

ANNA (*off stage*): Here it is, you blind bat.

GLAGOLYEV SR. (*falls off the bench*).

ANNA (*off stage*): You? Who are you? Don't hang about here! (*She shouts.*) Give it here, here!

SOPHIA (*comes running in looking pale and with her hair dishevelled*): I can't! This is too much! It's more than I can bear! (*She clutches at her bosom.*) My ruin or—happiness. It's so close here! He'll ruin me or—he's the herald of a new life. I welcome you. I bless you, my new life! It's settled!

VOYNITSEV (*off stage, shouting*): Look out!

Fireworks

SCENE TWO

A cutting in a forest. At the beginning of the cutting, on the left, a school building. Along the cutting, which stretches as far as the eye can see, is a railway track which turns right near the school. A row of telegraph poles. Night.
SASHA *sits at an open window and* OSIP *stands in front of it with a gun slung across his back.*

[OSIP: How did it happen, ma'am? Oh, I don't know. It was simple enough. I was walking along a forest path not very far from here and there she was, standing at the bottom of a small gulley: with her dress tucked up and scooping up water from the stream with a large burdock leaf. Kept scooping it up and drinking it, she did, and then she'd wet her head. I walks down to the stream, goes up close, and just keeps looking at her. Well, she pays no attention to me, just as if she was saying, 'Why should I pay any attention to a fool of a peasant like you?' 'Madam,' I says, 'I see your ladyship is enjoying a nice drink of cold water.' 'And what business is it of yours?' she says. 'Go back to where you came from.' She never even looks at me as she says it. Well, ma'am, I feels a little startled like. I feels ashamed of being a peasant and hurt, too, if you see what I mean. 'What are you staring at me for, you idiot?' she says. 'Never seen a human being before?' Then she gives me a knowing kind of look. 'Or do you like me?' she says. 'I like you a lot,' I says. 'Your ladyship is a fine figure of a woman. Very softhearted,' I says. 'Very beautiful. Never in all my life,' I says, 'did I see a woman more beautiful than you. Why,' I says, 'put beside you our village beauty, Manya, the policeman's daughter, is nothing but a horse, a camel. You're so delicate.' I says. 'If I was to kiss you,' I says, 'I'd drop dead on this very spot.' She laughs. 'Well,' she says, 'kiss me, if you want to.' When she says this, I feels hot all over. So I goes up to her, takes her gently by the shoulder, gives her a smacking kiss as hard as I can manage right here, on this very spot, cheek and neck at the same time.

SASHA (*bursts out laughing*): And what did she do?

OSIP: 'Well,' she says, 'now off with you. Don't forget to wash yourself more often,' she says, 'and see that you clean your fingernails.' So off I went.

SASHA: She's a bold one, she is. (*She gives* Osip *a plate of cabbage soup.*) There. Eat that. Sit down somewhere.

OSIP: I don't mind standing, ma'am. I'm no gentleman. Thanks very much for your kindness, ma'am. I'll repay you for it one day, I will.

SASHA: Take off your cap. It's sinful to eat with a cap on. And say your Grace, too.

OSIP (*takes off his cap*): Afraid I haven't been much of a religious man for a long time now. (*He eats.*) Since then I seem to have gone clean off my head. Would you believe it, ma'am? I can't eat, I can't sleep. She's always before my eyes. I've only to close them and there she stands—right there in front of me. Got myself into such a state I even thought of committing suicide. I did, you know, nearly drown myself, I felt so terrible. Why, I even thought of shooting her husband the general. And when she became a widow, I began carrying out all sorts of commissions for her. Shot partridges for her, caught quail, painted her summer house different colours. Once I even brought her a live wolf. Tried to please her in every way. Did everything she told me. If she'd told me to gobble myself up, I'd have gobbled myself up. Love, ma'am! You can't do nothing about it.

SASHA: Yes, I understand. When I fell in love with my husband, before I knew that he loved me too, I was terribly miserable. Several times I even prayed to God to let me die, sinful woman that I am.

OSIP: There you are. That's how one feels. (*He drinks what is left of the soup straight from the plate.*) There isn't any more soup, is there, ma'am? (*He hands her the plate.*)

SASHA (*goes out and after half a minute comes back to the window with a small saucepan*): I'm sorry there's no more soup, but you wouldn't like some potatoes, would you? Roasted in goose dripping.

OSIP: Thank you ma'am. (*He takes the saucepan and eats.*) I'm full up now. Anyway, so it went on and on, me walking about crazed like. I mean, me being in love with her ladyship. I kept on going to her house. Last year, after Easter, I brought her a hare. 'There you are, your ladyship,' I says to her, 'brought you this cross-eyed little fellow.' She takes it into her hands, strokes it, and asks me, 'Is it true what they say, Osip, that you are a brigand?' 'Gospel truth,' I says. 'People wouldn't be saying such things if it wasn't true.' So I told her everything. 'Must reform you,' she says. 'Off you go,' she says, 'on foot to Kiev, and from there to Moscow, and from Moscow to the Trinity monastery, and from the Trinity monastery to the New Jerusalem monastery, and from there come back home. Do it,' she says, 'and in a year's time you'll be a different man.' So I dressed up in beggar's clothes, slung a satchel over my shoulder and set off for Kiev. But nothing happened. I did reform, but not altogether . . . Lovely potatoes! You see, I fell in with a gang of thieves near Kharkov. Spent all my money on drink, got into a fight, and came back. Lost my passport even, I did. (*Pause.*) Now she won't take anything from me. Angry with me, she is.

SASHA: Why don't you go to church, Osip?

OSIP: I'd go only, you see, people will start laughing at me. 'Look at him,' they'll say, 'he's come to confess his sins.' Besides, I'm terrified to go near the church, even by day. Lots of people about—they're sure to kill me.

SASHA: Why, then, do you go about causing damage to poor folk?

OSIP: Why shouldn't I? That's something you wouldn't understand, ma'am. You're not the sort of person to know about such objectionable things. And what about your husband, ma'am? Don't he ever harm anyone?

SASHA: Of course he doesn't. If he does, it's against his will, by accident. He's a kind man.

OSIP: I must say I respects him more than anyone. The general's son, Mr. Voynitsev, I mean, is a stupid man. He isn't clever. Your brother isn't clever, either, though he's a doctor. But your husband's very brainy. Has he any civil service rank, ma'am?

SASHA: Of course! He is a collegiate registrar.

OSIP: Is he now? (*Pause.*) Aye, he's a fine man. A collegiate registrar, is he? Yes, a fine man. Except that there's not an ounce of goodness in him. He thinks everyone's either a fool or a boor. You can't treat people like that, can you? If I was a good man, I wouldn't behave like that. I'd be nice to fools and boors and thieves, for, you see, ma'am, they're the unhappiest people of the lot. It's people like that one ought to pity. There's not an ounce of goodness in him, I'm afraid. There's no pride in him, it's true, treats every man like he was his bosom friend, but no goodness, either. It's something you won't understand, ma'am. Thank you very much. I could eat such potatoes all my life. (*He hands back the saucepan.*) Thanks again, ma'am.

SASHA: Don't mention it.

OSIP (*sighs*): You're a nice woman, ma'am. Why do you feed me every time I come? Haven't got a drop of female malice in you, have you, ma'am? Religious too. (*He laughs.*) Never seen a woman like you before, ma'am. You're a saint, that's what you are. Pray for us sinners! (*He bows.*) Rejoice, Saint Alexandra!

SASHA: I think I can hear my husband coming.

OSIP: Don't try to fool me, ma'am. At this moment he's discussing affairs of the heart with the young mistress. A handsome man, your husband. Could have the whole female sex after him if he wanted to. A good talker, too. (*He laughs.*) Making up to the general's lady all the time, he is. Well, she'll send him off with a flea in his ear, she will. She won't give a damn about his being handsome. He'd be willing all right, I daresay, but she ...

SASHA: You're beginning to talk a lot of nonsense! I don't like it. I think you'd better go now.

OSIP: I'll be going in a minute. You should have been in bed long ago. Waiting up for your husband, I suppose?

SASHA: Yes.

OSIP: You're a good wife, ma'am. Platonov must have spent ten years looking for such a wife. Looked for her with candles and hired men. Managed to find one in the end, though. (*He bows.*) Well, good-bye, ma'am. Good night.

SASHA (*yawns*): Good-bye.

OSIP: I'm off. Going home. My home's anywhere where the earth is the floor and the sky is the ceiling, and goodness only knows where the walls and the roof are. Whom God has cursed lives in a house like that. It's a big house, but there's nowhere to lay one's head. The only good thing about it is that one hasn't to pay any land tax for it. (*He stops.*) Good night, ma'am. Come and see me sometimes. In the forest! Ask for Osip and every bird and lizard will tell you where to find me. Look how that stump is glowing! Just like a dead man risen from his grave. And there's another! My mother used to tell me that a sinner is buried under a glowing stump of a tree, and that it glows so that people will pray for him. A stump will be glowing over me, too. I, too, am a sinner. And there's a third one! Aye, there's lots of sinners in this world. (*He goes out and can be heard whistling for about two minutes.*)]

SASHA (*comes out of the schoolhouse with a candle and a book*): Michael is away a long time. (*Sitting down.*) Hope he won't catch a cold. These outdoor fêtes give you nothing but colds. [Yes, it's time I, too, went to bed. Where did I get to? (*She reads.*) 'It is certainly high time we again proclaimed those great eternal ideals of mankind, those immortal principles of freedom, which were the guiding stars of our fathers and which we, unfortunately, have betrayed.' What does it all mean? (*She thinks.*) I don't understand. I'd better go on. M-m-m-m-m. Leave out the preface. 'Zakhar Masoch' . . . What a funny name! Must be foreign. I'd better go on. Michael insists on my reading it, so I suppose I must read on. (*She yawns and reads.*) 'On a cheerful winter's evening . . .' Oh, I can skip that. A description. (*She turns over a number of pages and reads.*) 'It was difficult to make out who was playing and on what instrument. . . . The grand majestic sounds of an organ played by a man's iron hand suddenly changed to the tender sounds of a flute blown, it seemed, by a woman's lovely lips and at last died away . . .'] Sh-h-h-h. Someone's coming. (*Pause.*) Michael's footsteps . . . (*Blows out the candle.*) [At last! (*She gets up and shouts.*) Coo-e-e-e. One-two-one-two, left-right, left-right!

PLATONOV (*entering*): Just to spite you, right-right! But to tell the truth, my dear, it's neither right nor left. For when a man's drunk he has neither right nor left. All he knows is forward, backward, sideways and downwards.

SASHA: Come here, my darling drunkard. Come and sit here. (*She throws her arms round* Platonov's *neck.*) I'll teach you how to walk sideways and downwards. Sit down.

PLATONOV: Very well, let's sit down. (*He sits down.*) Why aren't you in bed, you infusoria, you?

SASHA: I don't feel like sleeping. (*She sits down next to him.*)] They've kept you late.

PLATONOV: Yes, late. Has the express gone through yet?

SASHA: Not yet. The goods train passed through about an hour ago.

PLATONOV: So it isn't two o'clock yet. How long have you been back?

SASHA: I was here already at ten. Little Nicholas was screaming his head off when I got back. I'm afraid I went away without saying good-bye. I hope they won't mind. Was there any dancing after I left?

PLATONOV: Yes. There was dancing, and there was supper, and there were also scenes. By the way, do you know? Did it happen while you were there? Old Glagolyev had a stroke.

SASHA: Not really!

PLATONOV: Yes. Your brother bled him and sang a requiem for him at one and the same time.

SASHA: But why? What was the matter with him? He looked so well.

PLATONOV: A mild stroke. Lucky for him, but not so lucky for that donkey of a son of his. They took him home. [There isn't a single party without some disgraceful scene. Such is our fate, I suppose.]

SASHA: I can imagine how frightened Anna and Sophie must have been! What a nice person Sophia is! I don't often see such pretty women. There's something special about her. (*Pause.*)

PLATONOV: Oh, stupid, disgusting . . .

SASHA: Why? What's happened?

PLATONOV: What have I done! (*He covers his face with his hands.*) I'm ashamed to think of it.

SASHA: What have you done?

PLATONOV: What have I done? Nothing that's any good, I can tell you. When have I ever done anything I haven't been ashamed of afterwards?

SASHA (*aside*): He's drunk, poor boy. (*To him.*) Let's go to bed.

PLATONOV: Vile as never before. How can I respect myself after that? There can be no greater misfortune than to lose one's self-respect. Good Lord! There's nothing in me to hold on to. Nothing to respect and love. (*Pause.*) Now you love me . . . I can't understand why. You must have found something in me that you can love. Do you love me?

SASHA: What a question! How could I not love you?

PLATONOV: I know, but please name me the good thing for which you love me so much! Show me the good thing you love in me.

SASHA: Why do I love you? You're a funny fellow tonight, Michael. How am I not to love you if you're my husband?

PLATONOV: So you only love me because I'm your husband?

SASHA: I don't understand you.

PLATONOV: You don't understand? (*He laughs.*) Oh, you darling little fool? Why aren't you a fly? With your brains, you'd be the most intelligent fly of all the flies. (*He kisses her on the forehead.*) What would happen to you if you did understand me, if you were not such an ignorant little pet? Would you have been so happy if you could grasp with your silly little head that I've nothing I can be loved for. Don't try to understand, my treasure. Don't try to find out if you want to go on loving me. (*He kisses her hand.*) My sweet little mate! Because of your ignorance I, too, am happy. I have a family, like everybody else . . . I have a family.

SASHA (*laughs*): You are funny!

PLATONOV: My treasure! My silly little darling of a wife! I oughtn't to have had you as my wife, but kept you under a bell glass on a table. And how did we manage, you and I, to bring little Nicholas into the world? You should be making little gingerbread men and not giving birth to little Nicholases.

SASHA: What silly nonsense you're talking, Michael!

PLATONOV: The Lord forbid that you should ever understand! Don't, don't understand! Let the earth be still resting on whales and the whales on pitchforks. Where would we get faithful wives, if there were no women like you, Sasha? (*He tries to kiss her.*)

SASHA (*resisting him*): Go away! (*Angrily.*) Why did you marry me if I'm so stupid? You should have got yourself a clever one! I didn't force you, did I?

PLATONOV (*laughs at the top of his voice*): So you know how to be angry, do you? Why, damn it all, it's a discovery in the field—

In what field? Anyway, it's quite a discovery, my darling. So you, too, know how to be angry? You're not pulling my leg?

SASHA: Come along, to bed with you! If you didn't drink, you wouldn't make any discoveries. Drunkard! A schoolmaster, too. You're not a schoolmaster, you're a pig! Go to bed! (*She slaps him on the back and goes into the schoolhouse.*)

PLATONOV (*alone*): Am I really drunk? I can't be. I haven't been drinking much. Still, my head's not quite right. (*Pause.*) Was I drunk when I was talking to Sophia? (*He thinks.*) No, I was not! I was *not*, unfortunately. I wasn't. I was as sober as a judge, damn it! (*He jumps to his feet.*) What wrong has her unhappy husband done me? Why should I have spoken with such contempt about her husband? I shall never forgive myself for this. I kept spouting to her like a silly young fool, showing off, putting on airs, boasting. (*Mimicking himself.*) 'Why didn't you marry a man who worked hard, who'd suffered for his beliefs?' Why the hell should she marry a man who worked hard and suffers for his beliefs? Why did you, crazy fool that you are, say something you didn't believe in? Dear Lord, she actually believed it! Listened to the crazy talk of a fool and dropped her eyes. Went all sentimental, poor thing. Overflowed with tenderness. How stupid it all is! How vile! How ridiculous! Oh, I'm sick of it all! (*He laughs.*) What a stupid selfish fool I am! Our merchants have been ridiculed as selfish fools, they were laughed at on the stage. Laughter through tears and tears through laughter. But who will laugh at me? When? Oh, it's too ridiculous for words! He takes no bribes. He doesn't steal. He doesn't beat his wife. Has decent ideas, but—he's a scoundrel! A ridiculous scoundrel! An egregious scoundrel! (*Pause.*) I must get away. Must ask the school inspector to transfer me to another job. I'll write to him this very day ...

[VENGEROVICH JR. *enters.*

VENGEROVICH JR. (*entering*): I see. This must be the school in which that half-baked sage is always asleep. Is he asleep now or is he abusing somebody as usual? (*Catching sight of* Platonov.) There he is, empty and hollow. Not asleep and not abusing anyone. Obviously in an abnormal state of mind. (*To* Platonov.) Haven't you gone to bed yet?

PLATONOV: As you see. But why have you stopped here? Allow me to bid you good night.

VENGEROVICH JR.: I'll be off in a minute. Enjoying your solitude? (*He looks round.*) Feeling yourself the Lord of Creation? On such a lovely night...

PLATONOV: Going home?

VENGEROVICH JR.: Yes. Father has driven off in our carriage and I'm forced to walk home. Enjoying yourself? It must be wonderful, don't you think, to drink champagne and then, plucking up courage, to indulge in a thorough self-examination. May I sit down beside you?

PLATONOV: You may.

VENGEROVICH JR.: Thank you. (*He sits down.*) I like to say 'thank you' for everything. It must be delightful to sit on the front steps here and feel that you are the complete master of your fate. Where's your girl friend, Platonov? Why these soft noises of the night, these whisperings of nature, this singing and chirring of the crickets only lack the sweet nothings lovers whisper to one another to transform it all into paradise! This flirtatious, timid breeze only wants the hot breath of your beloved to make your cheeks flush with happiness! The whispers of Mother Nature only want words of love. A woman! You look at me with amazement? Ha, ha! It isn't the sort of language you'd expect to hear from me? Well, no. It isn't. When I'm sober I shall blush a hundred times for having used this sort of language. However, why shouldn't I indulge in a little poetic chatter? Who can deny my right to indulge in it?

PLATONOV: No one.

VENGEROVICH JR.: Or do you think that this exalted language

does not accord with my position, my face? Isn't my face poetic?

PLATONOV: I'm afraid it isn't.

VENGEROVICH JR.: It isn't. Well, I'm very glad. Jews haven't got poetic faces. Nature has played a scurvy joke on us Jews. She hasn't given us poetic physiognomies. People are usually judged by their faces and because we do not possess a certain type of face, we are denied poetic feelings. They say the Jews have no poets.

PLATONOV: Who says?

VENGEROVICH JR.: They all say. But it's just dirty slander.

PLATONOV: Stop finding fault with everybody. Who says it?

VENGEROVICH JR.: They all say it. And yet, we've lots of poets. Not amateurs. Not like Pushkin or Lermontov but real ones. Auerbach, Heine, Goethe.

PLATONOV: Goethe is a German.

VENGEROVICH JR.: A Jew!

PLATONOV: A German!

VENGEROVICH JR.: A Jew! I know what I'm talking about.

PLATONOV: And I know what I'm talking about, too, but have it your own way. It's difficult to argue with a half-educated Jew.

VENGEROVICH JR.: Very difficult. (*Pause.*) But suppose they had no poets, what does it matter? If they have poets, it's all right. If they haven't, it's even better. A poet is a man of emotion. A man of emotion is, in the majority of cases, a parasite, an egoist. Did Goethe, as a poet, give a piece of bread to a single German proletarian?

PLATONOV: It's not original, young man. What matters is that he never took a piece of bread from a German proletarian. Besides, it's better to be a poet than a nobody. A million times better. However, we'd better say nothing more. Forget the pieces of bread, about which you haven't the slightest idea, and the poets whom your dehydrated soul doesn't understand, and you may as well leave me in peace, too.

VENGEROVICH JR.: I'm certainly not going to stir up your great heart, you splutterer. I'm not going to pull the eiderdown off your back. Go on sleeping. (*Pause*.) Just look at the sky! Yes, it's nice and peaceful here. There are only trees here. There aren't any satisfied, contented faces. Yes . . . But it's not for me the trees are whispering. And the moon doesn't look down as kindly on me as on Platonov here. It's looking coldly on me as if saying, 'You don't belong here. Away from this paradise! Get back to your dirty Jewish shop . . .' However, that's nonsense. I've been talking too much. Enough!

PLATONOV: Enough . . . Go home, young man. The longer you stay here, the more nonsense you'll talk and, as you have said yourself, you'll blush afterwards for all this nonsense. Go.

VENGEROVICH JR.: But I want to talk! (*He laughs*.) I'm a poet now.

PLATONOV: A man who's ashamed of his youth is no poet. Be young while you're young! Perhaps it's ridiculous and stupid but it's human.

VENGEROVICH JR.: I suppose so. But what nonsense it all is! You're a great eccentric, Platonov. You're all eccentrics here. You ought to have lived in the times of Noah. The general's widow is eccentric, and Voynitsev is eccentric. Incidentally, her ladyship is not so bad, anatomically speaking. What clever eyes she has! What beautiful fingers. Not bad at all . . . Lovely bosom, lovely neck . . . (*Pause*.) Why not? Am I worse than you? Just once in my life! If mere thoughts have so powerful an effect on my—er—spinal cord, then think what I'd have felt if she were to appear just now between those trees and beckon to me with her transparent fingers! Why, I'd melt away with bliss! Don't look at me like that. I'm stupid now. Just a young boy. However, who has the right to forbid me to be stupid at least once in my life? I should have liked to be stupid now just as a scientific experiment. Happy in your sense of the word. I am happy, too. It's nobody's business, is it? Well . . .

PLATONOV: But . . . (*He examines his watch chain.*)
VENGEROVICH JR.: However personal happiness is egoism.
PLATONOV: Yes, indeed. Personal happiness is egoism, and personal unhappiness is a virtue. What nonsense you do talk, though! What a wonderful chain! What marvellous seals! How it shines!
VENGEROVICH JR.: You're interested in this chain? (*He laughs.*) You're attracted by all this tinsel, this brilliance. (*Shakes his head.*) At the moment when you're preaching to me almost in verse, you're expressing your admiration for gold. Take this chain! Throw it away! (*He tears the chain off and throws it down on the ground.*)
PLATONOV: What a glorious sound! Its sound alone tells how heavy it is.
VENGEROVICH JR.: It's not only its weight that makes gold heavy. How lucky you are to be able to sit on these filthy steps! Here you do not experience the weight of this filthy gold. Oh, these golden chains, these golden fetters!
PLATONOV: These fetters are not very strong. Our fathers did not find it difficult to squander them on drink.
VENGEROVICH JR.: Think of the millions of unhappy, hungry and drunken people beneath the moon! When will the time come when the millions of those who sow so much and have nothing to eat cease to be hungry? When, I ask you? Why don't you reply, Platonov?
PLATONOV: Leave me alone. Do me a favour. I don't like bells that go on ringing unceasingly and to no purpose. I'm sorry, but do leave me. I want to go to bed.
VENGEROVICH JR.: Me a bell? I think it's you who are a bell.
PLATONOV: I'm a bell and you're a bell, the only difference being that I ring myself while you are rung by others. Good night. (*He gets up.*)
VENGEROVICH JR.: Good night. (*A clock in the school strikes two.*) Already two o'clock. One ought to be asleep at this time and

I'm still awake. Insomnia, champagne, excitement . . . An abnormal life—the ruin of your organism. (*Gets up.*) I believe I've already got a pain in my chest. Good night. I don't want to shake hands with you and I'm proud of it. You haven't the right to shake my hand.

PLATONOV: What nonsense! It's still one to me.

VENGEROVICH JR.: I hope our conversation, my—stupid talk, hasn't been overheard by anyone. I hope no one will ever hear of it. (*He goes upstage and then comes back.*)

PLATONOV: What do you want?

VENGEROVICH JR.: My chain must be here somewhere . . .

PLATONOV: There it is! (*He kicks the chain over to him.*) So you didn't forget it, did you? Look here, why not give up this chain to help an acquaintance of mine who belongs to the category of people who sow much and have nothing to eat. This chain will feed him and his family for many years. Shall I give it to him?

VENGEROVICH JR.: No, sir. I'd give it away with pleasure, but I'm afraid I can't. You see, it's a present. A souvenir.

PLATONOV: Yes, yes. Clear off!

VENGEROVICH JR. (*picks up the chain*): Leave me alone, please. (*He walks off to the back of the stage looking exhausted, sits down on the railway track and buries his face in his hands.*)

PLATONOV: The vulgarity of it! To be young and at the same time not to be a man of high principles. What utter depravity! (*He sits down.*) How we loathe people when we detect in them something that reminds us of our own impure past. Once I, too, was a little like him. Oh dear!] (*The sound of a horse's hooves is heard.*)

ANNA *comes in wearing a riding habit and carrying a hunting crop.*

PLATONOV: Anna!

ANNA: How can I see him? Shall I knock? (*Seeing* Platonov.) You're here? How fortunate! I knew you wouldn't be asleep yet. And indeed how is it possible to sleep now? God gave us the winter to sleep in. Good evening, you big, brawny man! (*She holds out her hand.*) Well? What's the matter? Your hand! (Platonov *holds out his hand.*) You're not drunk, are you?

PLATONOV: Damned if I know. I'm either sober or I'm as drunk as the most confirmed alcoholic. And what are you up to now? Taking your constitutional, my dear somnambula?

ANNA (*sits down beside him*): Yes. (*Pause.*) Yes, of course, my dear, dear Michael. (*She sings.*) How much happiness, how much torment . . . (*She bursts out laughing.*) What big, surprised eyes you've got, my dear friend! You've nothing to be afraid of.

PLATONOV: I'm not afraid—for me, at any rate. (*Pause.*) I can see your head's full of all sorts of nonsense.

ANNA: In my old age . . .

PLATONOV: Old women can be excused. They become senile. What kind of an old woman are you? You're as young as the summer in June. Life is in front of you.

ANNA: I want my life now and not in front of me. I'm young, Platonov. I'm terribly young. I feel it. It's like a wind blowing all over me. I'm devilishly young. Ugh! It's chilly! (*Pause.*)

PLATONOV (*jumping up*): I refuse to understand, to guess, or to suppose. I don't want anything. Go away! Call me a boor and leave me alone. I beg you. Why do you look at me like that? You . . . You think it over!

ANNA: I have thought it over.

[PLATONOV: Just think, proud, clever, beautiful woman! Where and why have you come? Good Lord . . .

ANNA: I didn't come, my darling, I rode over.]

PLATONOV: A woman of such intelligence, such beauty, a woman so young, and—come to me? I can't believe my eyes or my ears. She has come to conquer, to take the fortress by storm. I'm not a fortress! You haven't come here to conquer anything. I'm weak, terribly weak. Please, understand that.

ANNA (*gets up and walks up close to him*): Self-disparagement is worse than pride. What shall it be then, Michael? We'll have to end it somehow or other. You must agree that...

PLATONOV: I'm not going to end anything because I haven't begun anything.

ANNA: What a horrible philosophy! Aren't you ashamed to lie, darling? On such a night and under such a sky—to tell lies? Tell lies in the autumn if you must, when the ground's covered in mud and slush, but not now, not here. Not when you can be heard, when you are being watched. Look up at the sky, you funny fellow! See? Even the stars by their twinkling say that you're lying. My dear, stop all this nonsense. Be as good as all this is good. Do not break this calm by your own petty self. Chase away your demons from you! (*She puts her arm round him.*) There's no other man I could love as much as I love you! There's no woman you could love as you love me. Let's just take this love for ourselves and let others resolve the problems that torment you so. (*She kisses him.*) Let's just take this love for ourselves.

PLATONOV: It was only right that Odysseus should be sung to by the sirens, but I'm not King Odysseus, my siren. (*He embraces her.*) Oh, if only I could make you happy! How lovely you are! But I won't make you happy. I'll make you what I've made all the women who've thrown themselves at me. I'll make you unhappy!

ANNA: What a lot you think of yourself! Are you really such a terrible man, my Don Juan? (*She bursts out laughing.*) How handsome you are in the moonlight! Fascinating!

PLATONOV: I know the kind of man I am. Only those novels have happy endings in which I'm not the hero.

ANNA: Let's sit down—here! (*They sit down on the railway track.*) What else have you got to say, philosopher?

PLATONOV: If I were an honourable man, I'd leave you. I had a feeling that this would happen. I foresaw it. Why then, scoundrel, didn't I leave?

ANNA: Chase your demons away from you, Michael! [Don't poison yourself.] It's a woman who's come to you, not a wild beast. A long face, tears in the eyes . . . Really! If you don't want me I'll go away. Do you want me to go? I'll go and everything will be as it was before. Agreed? (*She bursts out laughing.*) Oh, you silly fellow! Take, snatch, grab! What more do you want? Smoke me to the end like a cigarette, squeeze me dry, cut me up into little pieces, be a man! (*She shakes him.*) Ridiculous fellow!

PLATONOV: But are you mine? Are you really meant for me? (*He kisses her hands.*) Go to another, my dear. Go to someone who's worthy of you.

ANNA: I wish to goodness you'd stop talking such nonsense! The whole thing's very simple: a woman who loves you and whom you love comes to you. The weather is lovely. What could be simpler? So what's the point of all this philosophy, all this temporizing? Not trying to show off, are you?

PLATONOV: Well . . . (*He stands up.*) But what if you've come to have a little fun with me, to go to bed with me, to play the fool? What then? You see, I'm not cut out for the part of a gigolo. I won't allow myself to be trifled with! You won't get rid of me with a few coppers as you got rid of lots of others. I'm too expensive for a casual affair. (*He clutches his head.*) To respect you, to love you, and at the same time—the pettiness, vulgarity, narrow-mindedness of it all—a plebeian pastime.

ANNA (*walking up to him*): You love me, you respect me, so why can't you stop worrying? Why are you haggling with me? Why are you saying all these vile things to me? Why all these 'ifs'? I love you. I told you so myself. And you know perfectly well that I love you. What more do you want? All I want is a little rest. (*She puts her head on his chest.*) A little rest. Please, understand me, Platonov. I want to rest. I want to forget myself. I don't want anything else. You don't know—you don't know how difficult life is for me and I—I want to live!

PLATONOV: But I'm not the man to give you a little rest.

ANNA: Stop philosophizing! Live! Everything lives, everything moves . . . Life is all around us. Let's live too! Let's solve our problems tomorrow. But now, tonight, let us live, live! Let us live, Michael! (*Pause.*) But, really, why am I carrying on like this? (*She bursts out laughing.*) How do you like that! I'm going down on my knees to him and he's being difficult.

PLATONOV (*seizing her by the hand*): Listen! For the last time! I'm begging you as an honest man—go away! For the last time—go away!

ANNA: Do you really mean it? (*She laughs loudly.*) You're not joking, are you? Don't be silly, I shall never leave you now. (*She throws her arms round his neck.*) Do you hear? I'm telling you for the last time: I won't let you go! Come what may, no matter what happens! Destroy me, ruin yourself, I'll have you still! Live! Tra-ta-ta-ta-ta, rah-rah-rah! Why are you trying to break away, you funny fellow? You're mine! Now you can talk as much as you like.

PLATONOV: For the last time . . . as an honest man . . .

ANNA: If I can't get you honourably, I'll take you by force! If you love me, love me and don't play the fool. Tra-ta-ta-ta-ta. [Bells of victory, ring out! Come to me, come to me!] (*She throws a black kerchief over his head.*) Come to me!

PLATONOV: To you? (*He laughs.*) [What a silly, frivolous woman you are!] You're asking for trouble. You'll be weeping, I tell you! I shall never be your husband, for you're not my sort, and I won't allow myself to be trifled with. We'll see who's going to trifle with whom. We'll see. You'll be weeping. Shall we go, then?

ANNA (*bursts out laughing*): Let's go! (*She takes his arm.*) Wait, someone's coming. Let's hide behind this tree. (*They hide behind the tree.*) Someone wearing a frock-coat. Not a peasant. [Why don't you write leading articles for newspapers? You'd do it beautifully. I'm not joking.]

TRILETSKY *enters.*

TRILETSKY (*goes to the schoolhouse and knocks at the window*): Sasha! Sister! Sasha darling!

SASHA (*opening the window*): Who's there? Is that you, Nicholas? What do you want?

TRILETSKY: You're not asleep yet? Let me stay the night, darling.

SASHA: Of course . . .

TRILETSKY: You can put me in the classroom. And, please, don't tell Michael I'm spending the night here. He won't let me sleep with his philosophy. I feel awfully dizzy. I see everything double. I'm standing in front of one window and I seem to be seeing two of them! Which one am I going to climb in through? What a nuisance! It's a good thing I'm not married, or I'd think I was a bigamist. Everything's double. You've got two heads on two necks. [Incidentally, I blew my nose over there by the felled oak tree, the one by the stream, you know it, don't you, and I must have dropped forty roubles out of my handkerchief. Do pick them up, darling, early in the morning. Find them and keep them.

SASHA: The carpenters will be sure to pick them up as soon as day breaks. How careless you are, Nicholas! Oh yes,] I nearly forgot. The shopkeeper's wife called. She wants you to go over there as quickly as possible. Her husband's been taken ill suddenly. Seems to have had a stroke. You'd better go quickly.

TRILETSKY: Oh, to hell with him! I don't feel like going there now. I've got awful pains in my head and in my belly myself. (*He climbs in through the window.*) Out of my way, please.

SASHA: Climb in quickly! You're standing on my dress. (*She shuts the window.*)

[PLATONOV: Someone else is coming, damn him!

ANNA: Wait!

PLATONOV: Don't hold me. I'll go if I want to. Who is it?

ANNA: Petrin and Shcherbuk.

PETRIN *and* SHCHERBUK *enter staggering and without their frockcoats.* PETRIN *wears a black top hat and* SHCHERBUK *a grey one.*

PETRIN: Three cheers for Petrin, Bachelor of Law! Hurrah! Which is the way? Where have we got to? What's this? (*He roars with laughter*.) Here, my dear fellow, is public education. Here they teach fools to forget God and swindle people. That's where we've got to. Yes, sir. Here, my dear fellow, that—hell, what's his name?—Platonov lives. A civilized man. Where is Platonov now, do you think, my dear fellow? Tell me frankly what you think. Don't be ashamed. Singing a duet with the general's widow. Oh Lord, Thy will be done . . . (*He shouts*.) Glagolyev's a fool. She sent him away with a flea in his ear and he had a stroke!

SHCHERBUK: I want to go home, my dear chap. I'm terribly sleepy. To hell with them all!

PETRIN: And what's happened to our frockcoats? We're going to spend the night at the stationmaster's and we haven't got our frockcoats. (*He roars with laughter*.) Have the servant girls taken them off? What a hell of a lover you are, my dear chap! The girls must have taken our coats off. (*He sighs*.) Oh, my dear fellow, so you've been drinking champagne, have you? You must be drunk now. And whose champagne have you been drinking? Why, mine! What you were drinking was mine and what you were eating was mine. The dress the general's widow was wearing was mine. The socks young Sergey is wearing are mine. Everything is mine. I've given them all I had! The heels on my old boots want mending, but I've given them all I had, squandered all my money on them, and what have I got in return? Go on, ask me, what have I got in return? A fig and disgrace! Yes, sir. Their lackey passes me over at table and tries to poke me with his elbow. She herself treats me like a pig . . .

PLATONOV: I can't stand any more!

ANNA: Wait! They'll be gone soon. What a swine that Petrin is! The lies he tells! And that spineless old idiot believes him.

PETRIN: They treat the Jew with more respect. He's at the head of the table and we're at the foot. Why? Because the Jew gives more money... And on his forehead are written the fatal words: For sale by public auction.

SHCHERBUK: That's by Nekrasov... I'm told Nekrasov's dead.

PETRIN: Very well then. Not another penny. Do you hear? Not another penny. Let the old man turn angrily in his grave. Let him have a row with... the gravediggers. Finished! I'm going to present the bills of exchange. Tomorrow! I'll drag her face in the mud, the ungrateful wretch!

SHCHERBUK: She's a count, a baron, she's got the face of a general. I'm just a Kalmuk. Nothing but a Kalmuk. I'm satisfied with Dunya. Let Dunya adore me... What an uneven road! There should be a highway here with telegraph poles and—and—bells. Ding, ding, ding. (*They go out.*)

ANNA (*comes out from behind the tree*): Have they gone?

PLATONOV: Yes, they've gone.]

ANNA (*taking him by the shoulders*): Shall we go?

PLATONOV: Yes, let's go. I'm coming, but if only you knew how reluctant I am! It's not me coming to you, but the devil who keeps hammering in my brain and saying, 'Go! Go!' It's not me but my weak body that's coming to you. Oh, how I would have tossed you aside were it not for this weak, gross body of mine!

ANNA? What a disgusting thing to say! (*She strikes* Platonov *with her hunting crop.*) Talk as much as you like but mind what you're saying! (*She walks away from* Platonov.) Come if you want to, if not—I don't care a damn! I'm not going to beg you on my knees. That's asking too much.

PLATONOV: Afraid it's too late to take offence. (*He follows her and takes her by the arm, but she jerks her arm away.*) I'll come anyway. It's too late to stop the devil in me... You're turning away? It's too late to take offence! We've put ourselves in such a position now that we cannot part however much our dignity's insulted. Please understand: if my conscience cannot accept your love, it's because it's convinced that you're making an irreparable mistake.

SASHA (*at the window*): Michael, Michael, where are you?

PLATONOV: Damn!

SASHA (*at the window*): Oh, there you are! Who are you with? (*She laughs.*) Anna! I hardly recognized you. You look so black! What is it you're wearing? Hullo!

ANNA: Hullo!

SASHA: You're wearing your riding habit? You're out riding then? How nice! It's such a lovely night. Let's go too, Michael.

ANNA: I've ridden enough, Sasha. I'm on my way home now.

SASHA: Well, of course, in that case. Do come in, Michael. I really don't know what to do. Nicholas is sick.

PLATONOV: Which Nicholas?

SASHA: My brother Nicholas. I expect he must have had too much to drink. Do come in. You too, Anna. I'll run down to the cellar and fetch some cream. Let's have a glass together. It's nice and cold.

ANNA: Thank you, but I'm going home now. (*To* Platonov.) You go in, I'll wait for you.

SASHA: I don't mind running down to the cellar. Come in, Michael. (*She disappears.*)

PLATONOV: I'd completely forgotten about her existence. She trusts me, doesn't she? Go... I'll get her to go to bed and then come.

ANNA: Don't be long.

PLATONOV: We've been lucky. There would have been hell to pay. Good-bye for now. (*He goes into the schoolhouse.*)

ANNA: What a surprise! I, too, had quite forgotten about her existence. (*Pause.*) It's cruel. Still, it's not the first time he's deceived the poor girl. Oh, well, if we have to sin, let's sin! No one but God will know, anyway. It's not for the first time. Damn! Now I have to wait till he gets her to bed. It will take an hour, if not more.

[VENGEROVICH JR. (*coming up to her*): Anna ... (*He drops on his knees before her.*) Anna ... (*He grasps her hand.*) Anna ...

ANNA: Who's that? Who are you? (*She bends over him.*) Who is it? You, Vengerovich? Is it you? What's the matter with you?

VENGEROVICH JR.: Anna! (*He kisses her hand.*)

ANNA: Go away. It's not nice. You—grown-up!

VENGEROVICH JR.: Anna!

ANNA: Stop clutching at me! Go away! (*She pushes him back by the shoulder.*)

VENGEROVICH JR. (*sprawling on the ground*): Oh Lord, it's stupid, stupid!]

OSIP (*coming in*): Comedians! It isn't you by any chance, your ladyship? (*He bows.*) What are you doing in our parts?

ANNA: Is that you, Osip? Good morning. Peeping? Spying? (*She takes him by the chin.*) Seen everything?

OSIP: Yes'm.

ANNA: And why are you so pale, eh? (*She laughs.*) Are you in love with me, Osip?

OSIP: It's as you like, ma'am.

ANNA: In love?

OSIP: Can't understand you, ma'am ... (*He weeps.*) I worshipped you like a saint. If you'd told me to go through fire, I'd have done it gladly.

[ANNA: Why didn't you go to Kiev?

OSIP: What do I want to go to Kiev for? I worshipped you like a saint. There was no one in the world holier than you.

ANNA: Don't talk such nonsense, you stupid fool! You'd better bring me some more of your hares. I'll accept them again. Well, good-bye.] Come and see me tomorrow and I'll give you some money. [You can then go to Kiev by train. All right?] Good-bye. And don't you dare touch Platonov, do you hear?

OSIP: From now on I'm not taking no orders from you, ma'am.

ANNA: Really? You wouldn't want me to go to a nunnery, would you? As if it's any of his business. There, there, don't cry.

You're not a little boy, are you? That'll do. When he's on his way to me, fire a shot.

OSIP: At him?

ANNA: No. In the air. Good-bye, Osip. A loud shot! Will you do it?

OSIP: I'll do it, ma'am.

ANNA: That's a clever boy.

OSIP: Only he won't go to you, he's with his wife now.

ANNA: Won't he? Good-bye, murderer! (*She runs off.*)

OSIP (*banging his cap on the ground and weeping*): It's finished! [It's all finished! May the earth swallow it up.

VENGEROVICH JR. (*lying on the ground*): What is he saying?]

OSIP: Saw the whole damn thing—heard it all, my eyes popping out of my head and a huge hammer beating at my ears. I heard everything! Well, what else can I do but kill him, seeing as how I'd like to tear him to pieces, crush every bone in his body between my teeth. (*He sits down on the mound with his back to the schoolhouse.*) I've got to kill him!

[VENGEROVICH JR.: What is he saying? Kill whom?]

PLATONOV (*pushing* Triletsky *out of the schoolhouse*): Get out! Off to the shopkeeper's this very minute! Run along!

TRILETSKY (*stretching himself*): I'd rather you'd knock me down with a big stick tomorrow than wake me now.

PLATONOV: You're a scoundrel, Nicholas. A scoundrel! Understand?

TRILETSKY: What can I do about it if God's made me like that?

PLATONOV: And what if the shopkeeper's dead already?

TRILETSKY: If he's dead, may he rest in peace, and if he's still continuing his struggle for existence, then you oughtn't to be saying such terrible things. I'm not going to the shopkeeper's. I want to go to sleep.

PLATONOV: You are going, you swine! You're going. (*He pushes him.*) I won't let you sleep. And, really, what's the matter with you? What do you think you're doing? What sort of man are you? Stuffing yourself all day long, wasting your time, idling away the best days of your life.

TRILETSKY: Stop pestering me. Sticking to me like a leech. Really!

PLATONOV: What kind of creature are you? Tell me that. This is terrible. What do you live for? Why don't you study? Why don't you keep up with medical studies? Why aren't you doing anything about it, you animal?

TRILETSKY: We'll discuss this highly interesting subject when I'm not so sleepy. Now let me go back to bed. (*He scratches himself.*) It's a bit too thick! For no reason at all—Get up you scoundrel! Professional ethics! To hell with them!

PLATONOV: What God are you worshipping, you strange creature? What kind of man are you? No, we shall never be of any use. Never!

TRILETSKY: Listen, my dear fellow, who gave you the right to thrust your cold paws into people's hearts. Such impudence is the absolute limit, my dear chap!

PLATONOV: Nothing will come of us, the lichens of the earth. We're done for, we're utterly worthless. (*He weeps.*) There's not a single man on whom I could look and be comforted. How vulgar, filthy, shabby everything is! Go away, Nicholas! Go!

TRILETSKY (*shrugging*): Crying? (*Pause.*) All right, I'll go to the shopkeeper. Do you hear? I'll go.

PLATONOV: Do as you like.

TRILETSKY: I'll go. I'm going now.

PLATONOV (*stamping his feet*): Clear off!

TRILETSKY: All right. You go to bed, Michael. It's not worth getting excited about. Good-bye. [(*He begins to go and stops.*) One last word before I go. Please advise all preachers, including yourself, that the sermons they make should conform to the preacher's deeds. If your eyes cannot find any comfort in looking at yourself, then you can't ask for any comfort for your eyes in looking at me. Your eyes, incidentally, look very beautiful in the moonlight. They scintillate like bits of green glass. And another thing. It's really a waste of time talking to you. You should be given a good beating, broken into pieces. I really should have nothing to do with you any more because of that poor girl. Oh, I wish I could tell you something, something you've never heard in your life before, but—I don't know how! I'm a bad duellist. That's jolly lucky for you. (*Pause.*) Good-bye.] (*He goes out.*)

PLATONOV (*clutching his head*): It's not only I who am vile. They're all vile. All! Lord, where are the decent people? I'm a nice one too. You mustn't go to her, she isn't yours! She belongs to someone else. You'll ruin her life, you'll corrupt her for good. [Go away from here. No! I shall go to her, I shall live here, I shall go on drinking, behaving like a pagan. Depraved, stupid, drunk! Always drunk. A fool of a mother, a drunkard of a father, and here I am! Father, mother! Father . . . Oh, I wish your bones were crushed in your graves as you've crushed my poor life by your drunkenness and your folly. (*Pause.*) No, what was I saying? May God forgive me. May they rest in peace. (*He stumbles over* Vengerovich Jr.) Who is this?

VENGEROVICH JR.: Wild, disgusting, infamous night!

PLATONOV: Oh, it's you! Go and write this wild night down in your stupid diary with the ink of your father's conscience. Get out!

VENGEROVICH JR.: Yes, I will write it down. (*He goes out.*)

PLATONOV: What was he doing here? Eavesdropping? (*To* Osip.) Who're you? What are you doing here, freebooter? Been eavesdropping too? Get out! No, wait. Run after Vengerovich and take his chain off him.

OSIP (*getting up*): What chain?

PLATONOV: He's wearing a large gold chain across his chest. Catch him and take it off. Quick! (*Stamping his feet.*) Quick! Or you won't catch him. He's running like mad now towards the village.

OSIP: And you're off to the general's widow?

PLATONOV: Run quickly, you scoundrel! Don't hit him, just take his chain. Away with you! What are you standing there for? Run!

OSIP *runs off.*

PLATONOV (*after a pause*): Shall I go?... To go or not to go. (*He sighs.*) To go... I'll go and strike up that long, essentially boring and ugly song.] I thought I went about clad in strong armour, but what actually happens? A woman utters one word and a storm is let loose within me. Others are interested in world problems, I'm only interested in women. All my life was just one damn woman after another. For Caesar it was the Rubicon, for me it is woman. I'm a womanizer, nothing more. I shouldn't have minded it had I not fought against it. But I do fight against it. I'm weak, terribly weak.

[SASHA (*at the window*): Michael, are you there?

PLATONOV: Yes, my poor treasure.

SASHA: Come inside.

PLATONOV: No, Sasha. I'd like to stay a little longer in the fresh air. My head's bursting. Go to sleep, my angel.

SASHA: Good night. (*She shuts the window.*)

PLATONOV: It's hard to deceive someone who believes blindly in you. It threw me into a sweat and made me blush... I'm going...] (*He is about to go off when* Katya *and* Yakov *meet him as they come towards him.*)

KATYA (*to* Yakov): Wait here. I won't be long. [I'll only get a book. Mind, don't go away.] (*She goes towards* Platonov.)

PLATONOV (*seeing* Katya): You? What are you doing here?

KATYA (*frightened*): [Oh, it's you, sir.] I'm looking for you, sir.

PLATONOV: [Is it you, Katya?] All, from the mistresses to the maids, all are nightbirds. What do you want?

KATYA (*lowering her voice*): I've got a letter for you from my mistress.

PLATONOV: [What are you talking about?] Which mistress?

KATYA (*lowering her voice still more*): Sophia Voynitsev, sir.

PLATONOV: Good Lord, have you gone off your head? [Go and pour some cold water over yourself. Get out of here!]

KATYA (*handing him the letter*): Here it is, sir.

PLATONOV (*snatching the letter*): A letter . . . a letter . . . What letter? Couldn't you have brought it in the morning? (*He opens it.*) I can't see to read it.

KATYA: Mistress would like a reply as soon as possible.

PLATONOV (*striking a match*): The devil brings you here! (*He reads.*) 'I am taking the first step. Come, let's take it together. I am reborn. Come and take me. I am yours.' What the hell? . . . Like a telegram. (*He goes on reading.*) 'Shall wait till four at the pagoda by the four pillars. Husband drunk, went off hunting with young Glagolyev. All yours. S.' This is all I needed. Good Lord, this is all I needed!

(*To* Katya.) [What are you looking at?

KATYA: I can't help looking if I've got a pair of eyes, can I, sir?

PLATONOV: Pluck them out! Are you sure this letter is for me?

KATYA: Yes, it's for you, sir.

PLATONOV: You're lying.] Get out of here!

KATYA: Yes, sir. (*She goes out with* Yakov.)

PLATONOV (*after a pause*): [Well, so there you have the consequences. You're in a proper mess now, old boy. You've ruined a woman's life, the life of a living creature, for nothing, without any need, senselessly. It's my damned tongue! It's brought me to all this! What am I to do now? Well, clever head, try to think of something! Curse yourself. Tear your hair. (*He thinks.*)] I must go away. I must go away at once and never show my face here again [till the Day of Judgment. Double quick, out of here, to the four corners of the earth, under the iron discipline of poverty and hard work! A hundred times better to eke out a miserable living than put up with this sort of life!] (*Pause.*) I'll go away. But—does Sophy really love me? Does she? (*He laughs.*) But why? How strange and mysterious everything is in this world. (*Pause.*) Strange. Is it possible that that beautiful, marble-like woman with her wonderful hair is capable of falling in love with a poverty-stricken crank like me? Does she really love me? Incredible! (*He lights a match and reads over the letter again.*) Yes . . . Me? Sophy? (*He laughs.*) Loves me? (*Clutching at his chest.*) Happiness! Why, this is happiness! This is my happiness! This is a new life, with new people, new scenery! [I'm coming! Double quick to the pagoda near the four pillars.] Wait for me, my Sophia! You were mine, and you will be mine again! (*He starts walking, then stops.*) I won't go. (*Walking back to the schoolhouse.*) Destroy my family? (*Shouts.*) Sasha, I'm coming in, open the door! (*Clutching his head.*) I won't go. I won't go . . . I won't go! (*Pause.*) I will—I will go. (*He starts walking.*) Go on, smash up, trample down, defile . . . (*He bumps into* Voynitsev *and* Glagolyev Jr. *who run in with guns slung across their backs.*)

VOYNITSEV: Here he is! Here he is! (*Embracing* Platonov.) Come, let's go shooting.

PLATONOV: No . . . Let me go.

VOYNITSEV: Why are you trying to tear yourself away from me? (*He laughs.*) I'm drunk, drunk! For the first time in my life! Lord, I'm so happy. My dear friend! (*He embraces* Platonov.) Are you coming with us? She sent me off. Told me to shoot some game for her.

GLAGOLYEV JR.: Come, let's go quickly. It's getting light already.

VOYNITSEV: Have you heard what we're planning to do? Don't you think it's a stroke of genius? We're thinking of putting on *Hamlet*. Word of honour! We'll show them such acting that even the devils will go green with envy! (*He laughs loudly.*) How pale you are! Are you drunk too?

PLATONOV: Let me go . . . I'm drunk.

VOYNITSEV: Wait. It's my idea. Tomorrow we shall start painting the scenery. I shall play Hamlet, Sophy—Ophelia, you—Claudius, Triletsky—Horatio. Oh, I'm so happy! Happy and contented. Shakespeare, Sophy, you and Mother. I don't need anyone else. Sorry, Glinka too, of course. Nothing else. I am Hamlet.

    Could you on this mountain leave to feed,
    And batten on this moor? Ha! Have you eyes?
    You cannot call it love...

(*He laughs loudly*.) Not such a bad Hamlet, am I?

PLATONOV (*tears himself away and runs*): Scoundrel! (*He runs off*.)

VOYNITSEV: Good heavens, he *is* drunk. Drunk as a lord! (*He laughs*.) What do you think of our friend?

GLAGOLYEV JR.: Sozzled! Let's go.

VOYNITSEV: Let's go. 'Give me that man that is not passion's slave... Ophelia, nymph, in thy orisons be all my sins remembered!' (*He goes off. The sound of an approaching train can be heard.*)

OSIP (*runs in [with the chain*]: Where is he? (*Looking round*.)] Where is he? Gone? Not here? (*He whistles*.) Mr. Platonov! Mr. Platonov! Oi! (*Pause*.) Not here? (*He runs up to the window and knocks.*) Mr. Platonov! Mr. Platonov! (*He breaks the window*.)

SASHA (*at the window*): Who's there?

OSIP: Call Mr. Platonov, ma'am. Quick!

SASHA: What's happened? He's not at home.

OSIP (*shouts*): Not at home? Then he's with the general's lady. She was here and she called him to go back with her. Everything's lost. He's gone to the general's lady, damn him!

SASHA: You're lying!

OSIP: May I drop dead if he hasn't gone to her. I heard and saw everything. They were embracing and kissing here.

SASHA: You're lying!

OSIP: Let neither my father nor my mother see the kingdom of heaven if I'm lying. He has gone off to the general's lady. He's left his wife. Run after him, ma'am. No, no, it's too late. Everything's lost! And you're the unhappy one now. (*He takes his gun from his shoulder.*) She gave me my orders for the last time and I shall carry them out for the last time. (*He fires a shot in the air.*) Let her meet him! (*He flings his gun down on to the ground.*) I'll cut his throat, ma'am. (*He jumps over the mound and sits on a tree stump.*) Don't worry, ma'am, don't worry . . . I'll cut his throat. Don't doubt it for a moment. (*The lights of an approaching train appear.*)

SASHA (*comes out in her nightdress with her hair down*): He's gone . . . He has deceived me. (*She sobs.*) I'm done for. Kill me, Lord, after this! (*The train's whistle is heard.*) I'll throw myself under the train. I don't want to live. (*She lies down on the rails.*) Deceived me! Kill me, O Mother of God. (*Pause.*) Forgive me, O Lord! (*She shouts.*) Nicholas! (*She gets up on her knees.*) My son! Save me! Save me! The train's coming! Save me!

OSIP *runs up to* SASHA.

SASHA (*collapses on the rails*): Oh!
OSIP (*picks her up and carries her towards the schoolhouse*): I'll cut his throat . . . don't you worry.

The train passes through.

END OF ACT TWO

ACT THREE

A room in the school. Doors on the right and left. A cupboard with crockery, a chest of drawers, an old upright piano, chairs, a sofa upholstered in American cloth, a guitar, etc. The whole place is in utter confusion.

        PLATONOV *is asleep on the sofa by the window.*
        His face is covered with a straw hat.

SOPHIA (*waking* Platonov): Platonov! Michael! (*She pushes him.*) Wake up, darling! (*Taking the hat from his face.*) How can you cover your face with such a filthy old hat? Dear me, what a filthy mess! How untidy you are! Lost his studs, sleeps with a bare chest, unwashed, in a dirty nightshirt. Michael! I'm speaking to you. Get up!

PLATONOV: Eh?

SOPHIA: Wake up!

PLATONOV: Not now. Oh, all right.

SOPHIA: You've slept long enough. Please, get up!

PLATONOV: Who is it? Is it you, Sophia?

SOPHIA (*holding a watch in front of his eyes*): Look at the time!

PLATONOV: All right . . . (*He lies down again.*)

SOPHIA: Platonov!

PLATONOV: Well? What do you want? (*Rising.*) Well?

SOPHIA: Look at the time!

PLATONOV: What's up? You again, Sophy, with your stupid fancies.

SOPHIA: Yes, it's me again, with my stupid fancies, my dear Michael. Take a look at my watch, please. What's the time now?

PLATONOV: Half past seven.

SOPHIA: Half past seven. And have you forgotten our arrangement?

PLATONOV. What arrangement? Do explain, Sophia. I'm not in the mood today to make jokes or to solve idiotic riddles.

SOPHIA: What arrangement? Have you forgotten? What's the matter with you? Your eyes are red, and you look all crumpled. Are you ill? (*Pause.*) Our arrangement was that we should both be at the hut at six o'clock this morning. Forgotten? It's long past six.

PLATONOV: What else?

SOPHIA (*sitting down beside him*): Aren't you ashamed? Why didn't you come? You promised most faithfully.

PLATONOV: I would have kept my promise if I hadn't fallen asleep. You can see I've been sleeping, can't you? So why are you badgering me?

SOPHIA (*shaking her head*): What a dishonourable man you are! Why are you looking so angrily at me? Dishonourable so far as I'm concerned, at any rate. Just think, have you ever been on time even once? How many times have you broken your promises to me!

PLATONOV: I'm very glad to hear it.

SOPHIA: That's not clever, Platonov. You ought to be ashamed of yourself. Why is it that when I am with you, you no longer behave decently? You cease to be intelligent, you no longer seem to be yourself. Why these plebeian airs so unworthy of the man to whom I owe the salvation of my soul? You behave like a sort of ogre to me. Not a kind look, not a gentle word, not a single word of love. I come to see you and you reek of vodka, you're not dressed decently, your hair isn't brushed, you're rude, you don't even listen to what I say.

PLATONOV (*jumping up and walking up and down the stage*): There she goes again!

SOPHIA: Are you drunk?

PLATONOV: What business is that of yours?

SOPHIA: How charming! (*She weeps.*)

PLATONOV: Women!!

SOPHIA: Don't you talk about women to me. [You talk to me about them a thousand times a day. I'm sick of it. (*She gets up.*) What are you doing to me? Do you want to kill me? I'm a sick woman because of you. Thanks to you I have a pain in my chest—day and night. Don't you see it all? Don't you want to know about it? You hate me!] If you loved me, you wouldn't dare treat me like this. [I'm not just some provincial miss for you! I'm no coarse, uncouth creature. I'm not going to let a man like you ... (*She sits down.*) For God's sake.] (*She weeps.*)

PLATONOV: That's enough.

SOPHIA: You're killing me! It's hardly three weeks since that night, and I'm as thin as a rake. Where's the happiness you promised me? What will be the end of all these antics of yours? Think, you clever, noble, honest man! Think Platonov, before it's too late! [Think now—now! Sit down on this chair, put everything out of your mind and just think of one thing: what are you doing to me?]

PLATONOV: I don't know how to think. (*Pause.*) You'd better think it out yourself! (*He walks up to her.*) [Yes, you think I've deprived you of your family, your comforts, your future. Why? For what reason? I've robbed you as if I were your worst enemy. What can I give you in return? How can I repay you for your sacrifices?] All I know is that this illicit affair of ours is your misfortune, your ruin, your downfall! (*He sits down.*)

SOPHIA: I've given myself to him, and he dares call our relationship an illicit affair!

PLATONOV: Now is hardly the time to find fault with every word I utter. You look upon our relationship in one way and I in another. I've ruined you, and that's all there is to it. And not only you. Wait till you hear the tune your husband will sing when he finds out.

SOPHIA: Are you afraid he might make things unpleasant for you?
PLATONOV: No, I'm not afraid of that. I'm afraid that we may kill him.
SOPHIA: Then why did you come to me that night, you spineless coward, if you knew that we were going to kill him?
PLATONOV: A little less emotion, please! You won't make any impression on me with your heart-rending appeals. And why did *you* . . . However . . . (*He waves his hand.*) Talking to you only brings on a flood of tears.
SOPHIA: Yes, yes. I never wept before I became your mistress. Well, go on, be afraid, tremble! He already knows.
PLATONOV: What did you say?
SOPHIA: He knows already.
PLATONOV (*rising*): He does?
SOPHIA: Yes, he does. I told him everything this morning.
PLATONOV: You're joking . . .
SOPHIA: Turned pale, have you? One ought to hate you, not love you. I must be mad. I don't know why—why I love you. Yes, he knows already. (*Shaking him by his sleeve.*) Why don't you tremble? He knows everything. I tell you, he knows everything. Tremble!
PLATONOV: It's impossible. It can't be. (*Pause.*)
SOPHIA: He knows everything. He had to know one day, hadn't he?
PLATONOV: [Why then are you trembling? How did you tell him? What did you say to him?]
SOPHIA: I told him that I was already . . . that I can't . . .
PLATONOV: And he?
SOPHIA: He was just like you—frightened! Oh, how insufferable your face is at this moment!
PLATONOV: What did he say?
SOPHIA: At first he thought I was joking, but when he realized I wasn't, he turned pale, began to sway, burst into tears, crawled on his knees . . . his face was as repulsive as yours is now.

PLATONOV: What have you done, you detestable woman! (*Clutching his head.*) You've killed him! And you can, you dare talk about it so cold-bloodedly! You've killed him? Did you ... did you mention my name?

SOPHIA: Yes. What else did you expect me to do?

PLATONOV: And he?

SOPHIA (*jumping up*): Have you no shame, Platonov? You don't know what you're saying. According to you, shouldn't I have spoken?

PLATONOV: Of course you shouldn't. (*He lies down on the sofa, face downwards.*)

SOPHIA: What are you saying, you honest man?

PLATONOV: It would have been much more honest not to tell him than to kill him. We have killed him. He wept, crawled on his knees. Good Lord! (*Jumps up.*) Unhappy man! But for you, he would never have found out about our affair.

SOPHIA: It was my duty to tell him. I am an honest woman.

PLATONOV: Do you realize what you've done by telling him? You've parted from your husband for ever.

SOPHIA: Yes, for ever. What else? Platonov, you're beginning to talk like a—blackguard!

PLATONOV: For ever. What's going to happen to you when we part? And part we shall soon. You'll be the first to realize that you've made a mistake. You'll be the first whose eyes will be opened, and it will be you who will leave me. (*He waves his hand.*) However, do as you like, Sophy. You're more honest and more intelligent than I, so take charge of all this quite unnecessary mess. Do as you like. Bring me back to life if you can. Put me back on my feet. Only, for God's sake, do it quickly or I'll go mad!

SOPHIA: We leave tomorrow.

PLATONOV: Yes, yes. Let's go away! Only quickly!

SOPHIA: I must take you away from here. I've written to my mother about you. We'll go to her.

PLATONOV: Anywhere you like! Do as you think best.
SOPHIA: Michael, please understand. It's a new life we're embarking on. Do as I tell you. Let me arrange everything. My head is clearer than yours. Trust me, my dear. I'll put you back on your feet. I'll take you to a place where there's more light, where there isn't any of this squalor, this dust, this idleness, this filthy nightshirt. I'll make a man of you. I'll give you happiness! Please, Michael, understand. (*Pause.*) I'll make you love your work. We'll be decent people, Michael. We shall eat our own bread. We shall live by the sweat of our brows. We shall have calloused hands. (*She lays her head on his chest.*) I shall work, Michael.
PLATONOV: Where will you work? There are women who're not like you, who are much stronger than you and they're lying about like sheaves of corn, unable to find any work. [You don't know how to work. And, anyway, what kind of work will you do? Our present position is such, Sonya, that it would be more useful to think clearly than to console oneself with illusions. However, do as you like.]
SOPHIA: You'll see. There may be women who are not like me, but I'm stronger than they. Have faith, Michael. [I'll light the way for you. You have brought me back to life and I'll be grateful to you all my life.] Do we leave tomorrow? Yes? I'll go and start packing at once. You, too, must get ready. Come to the hut at ten o'clock and bring your things with you. You will come, won't you?
PLATONOV: I will.
[SOPHIA: Give me your word of honour that you'll come.
PLATONOV: Please, I said I'd come.]
SOPHIA: On your word of honour?
PLATONOV: On my word of honour . . . I swear.
SOPHIA (*laughs*): I believe you. Why not come earlier? I'll be ready before ten. We'll be off tonight. We'll turn over a new leaf, Michael! You don't understand your own good fortune,

you silly man! Why, it's our happiness, our life! Tomorrow you'll be a different man—fresh, new! We shall breathe new air, new blood will start coursing in our veins. (*She bursts out laughing.*) Away, decrepit man! Here, take my hand! Hold it tight! (*She gives him her hand.* Platonov *kisses it.*) My big clumsy bear! I'll wait for you. Don't brood. Good-bye for the present. It won't take me long to get ready. (*She kisses him.*)

PLATONOV: Good-bye. Ten or eleven?

SOPHIA: Ten. Come earlier, if you can. Good-bye. Put on some decent clothes for the journey. (*She laughs.*) I have some money. We'll have supper on the way. Good-bye! I'll go and get ready. Cheer up! I expect you at ten. (*She runs off.*)

PLATONOV (*after a pause*): It's not a new tune. I've heard it a hundred times before. [(*Pause.*) I must write a letter to him and to Sasha. Let them have a good cry. They'll forgive and forget. Good-bye, Voynitsevka. Good-bye, all. Sasha and Anna.] (*He opens the cupboard.*) Tomorrow I shall be a new man—I don't think! What am I going to put my clothes in? I haven't a suitcase ... (*He pours himself a drink.*) [Good-bye, school! (*He drinks.*) Good-bye, children! You'll never see your bad but kind Platonov again. Did I drink just now? Why? Mustn't drink any more. It's for the last time. I'll write to Sasha ... (*He lies down on the sofa.*)] Sophy really believes ... Blessed are they that believe. (*He drinks.*) You can laugh, Anna! And she'll laugh, too! Roar with laughter! Good Lord, I believe there was a letter from her ... Where is it? (*He picks up a letter from the window.*) The hundredth, if not the two hundredth letter after that wild night ... (*He reads.*) 'You, Platonov, who do not answer my letters, are an indelicate, cruel, and stupid oaf. If you leave this letter, too, unanswered and don't come to see me, I shall pay a call on you myself, damn you! [I shall wait all day for you. It's silly, Platonov. One would think you were ashamed of that night. Let's forget it, if that's what you want.] Sergey and Sophia are behaving abominably. What an end to their honeymoon! And it's all because they haven't got that eloquent, self-conceited chump with them. You are that self-conceited chump. Good-bye!' (*Pause.*) What handwriting! Precise, bold. Commas, full stops, no spelling mistakes . . . A woman who can write so correctly is a rare phenomenon. (Marko *enters*.) I shall have to write to her or for all I know she may come. (*Catching sight of* Marko.) Another phenomenon. Come in! Who are you looking for? (*He gets up.*)

MARKO: I've come to see you sir. (*He takes a summons out of his satchel.*) A summons for you, sir.

PLATONOV: Oh? That's nice. [What sort of summons? Who sent you?

MARKO: The Justice of the Peace, sir.

PLATONOV: Oh? What does the Justice of the Peace want with me?] Give it here. (*Taking the summons.*) What can it be? An invitation to a christening? The old sinner is as prolific as a locust. (*He reads.*) 'To the defendant in the case of an assault committed upon the person of Maria Grekov, daughter of Councillor of State . . .' (*He laughs.*) Well, I'm hanged! Bravo! Damn it! Bravo, bedbug ether! [When will the case be heard? The day after tomorrow? I'll be there, I'll be there. Tell him, old man, that I'll be there.] Damn clever girl. Well done! She should have done it long ago!

MARKO: Will you sign for it, sir?

PLATONOV: Sign? By all means. [You know, old man, you look terribly like a wounded duck.

MARKO: Begging your pardon, sir, but I don't look like that at all.

PLATONOV (*sitting down on the table*): What do you look like then?

MARKO: I'm in the image and likeness of God, sir.

PLATONOV: I see. You're an old soldier, aren't you?

MARKO: Yes, sir. I was discharged after the Sevastopol campaign, sir. Spent four years in hospital, I did, in addition to my army service. Non-commissioned officer, sir. Sergeant of artillery.

PLATONOV: I see. Did you have good guns?

MARKO: Usual ones. Round bore.

PLATONOV: Can I sign with a pencil?

MARKO: Yes, sir. Just say, received this summons, and put your name, patronymic and surname, sir.

PLATONOV (*getting up*).] Here you are. [Signed five times. Well, how's your Justice of the Peace? Still gambling?

MARKO: Yes, sir.

PLATONOV: From five o'clock in the afternoon till five o'clock in the afternoon?

MARKO: Yes, sir.

PLATONOV: Hasn't lost his chain of office yet, has he?

MARKO: No, sir.

PLATONOV: Tell him ... No, don't tell him anything. I don't suppose he pays his gambling debts. The fool plays cards, runs into debt, and has a whole crowd of children to provide for ... What a clever girl, damn her! Didn't expect it. Didn't expect it at all. Who are the witnesses? Who else have you got summonses for?

MARKO (*reads*): Doctor Nicholas Triletsky ...

PLATONOV: Triletsky! (*He laughs.*) That should be funny! And who else?

MARKO: Mr. Cyril Glagolyev, Mr. Alphonse Schrifter, retired cornet of the guards Maxim Aleutov, son of Regular State Councillor Ivan Tallier, Mr. Sergey Voynitsev, graduate of St. Petersburg Niversity.

PLATONOV: Is that how it's spelt—Niversity?

MARKO: No, sir.

PLATONOV: Then why do you read it like that?

MARKO: Because of my ignorance, sir. (*Reads.*) Uni ... uni ... niversity—his wife, Mrs. Sophia Voynitsev—Mr. Isaac Vengerovich, student of Kharkov University. That's the lot, sir.

PLATONOV: I see. So it's the day after tomorrow and we have to leave tomorrow. Pity. I can imagine what fun such a trial would be! What a nuisance! I should have liked to give her the pleasure . . . (*Walking up and down the stage.*) A nuisance!

MARKO: No tip, sir? I had to walk five miles.

PLATONOV: A tip? No, I won't give you a tip, my dear fellow, but I'll give you some tea instead. That will be cheaper for me and, what's more, it will keep you sober. (*He takes a tea caddy out of the cupboard.*) Come here. It's good, strong tea . . . Strong, though not forty proof. What am I to put it in for you?

MARKO (*holding out his pocket*): Put it in my pocket, sir.

PLATONOV: Straight into the pocket! Won't it smell?

MARKO: Put it in, put it in, sir. Don't worry.

PLATONOV (*pouring the tea leaves into his pocket*): Is that enough?]

MARKO: Thank you kindly, sir.

[PLATONOV: What a nice old man you are. I'm fond of old soldiers like you. Fine fellows. But even among you one sometimes comes across such horrors . . .

MARKO: There are all sorts, sir. God alone is without sin.] Good-bye, sir.

PLATONOV: Wait . . . One moment . . . (*He sits down and writes on the summons.*) 'I kissed you then because . . . because I felt irritated and I did not know what I wanted. But now I'd kiss you as though you were something sacred! I admit I was beastly to you. I am beastly to everybody. I'm afraid we shan't meet in court. Tomorrow I'm leaving for good. I hope you will be happy and that at least you will be fair to me. Do not forgive me!' (*To Marko.*) Do you know where Miss Grekov lives?

MARKO: Yes, sir. It's about ten miles from here if you cross the river at the ford.

PLATONOV: That's right. [She lives in Zhilkovo.] Take this letter to her and you'll get three roubles. Give it to the young lady personally. [There's no reply. If she tries to give you one, don't take it. Take it to her today. Right now! Take it to her first and then deliver your summonses.] (*He walks up and down the stage.*)

MARKO: [I understand, sir.
PLATONOV: What else? Oh, yes. Tell everyone that I apologized to Miss Grekov, but that she would not accept my apology.
MARKO: I understand, sir.] Good day, sir.
PLATONOV: Good-bye, friend. Take care of yourself.

Marko goes out.

(*Alone.*) Now I'm quits with Mary. [She'll give me a bad name throughout the whole of the province. Serves me right.] It's the first time in my life a woman has punished me. (*He lies down on the sofa.*) You treat them like dirt and they fling themselves on your neck. Sophia, for instance. (*He covers his face with his handkerchief.*) I was as free as the wind and now I lie here and—dream! Love! ... Amo, amas, amat! Got myself into a proper mess. Ruined her and did myself no great service either. (*He sighs.*) Poor Voynitsev! And Sasha? Poor darling. How will she be able to carry on without me? She'll waste away and die ... She's left me. Suspected the truth and left me, taking our child and without uttering a single word. Gone away after that night. If only I could have said good-bye to her ...

ANNA (*at the window*): May I come in? Hey! Anyone in?
PLATONOV: Anna! (*He jumps up.*) What can I say to her? What has she come here for I'd like to know. (*He straightens his clothes.*)
ANNA (*at the window*): May I come in? I'm coming in! Do you hear?
PLATONOV: [She's here! I can't possibly not let her in, can I?] (*He combs his hair.*) I wish I knew how to get rid of her. I'd better have a drink before she comes in. (*He quickly opens the cupboard.*) And what the hell does she want? (*He drinks quickly.*) I hope she doesn't know anything. What if she does? I shall look an awful fool!
ANNA (*comes in while* Platonov *is slowly closing the cupboard.*) How do you do?
PLATONOV: It won't close ... (*Pause.*)

ANNA: You there! Good morning!
PLATONOV: Oh, it's you Anna? I'm sorry, I didn't notice. This damn door won't close . . . (*He drops the key and picks it up again.*)
ANNA: Come over to me! Leave the cupboard alone! Leave it!
PLATONOV (*coming up to her*): Hullo!
ANNA: Why won't you look at me?
PLATONOV: I'm too ashamed. (*He kisses her hand.*)
ANNA: What of?
PLATONOV: Everything.
ANNA: I see. You haven't seduced anyone, have you?
PLATONOV: Yes, something like that.
ANNA: Well, well! And who's the girl?
PLATONOV: I shan't tell you.
ANNA: [Let's sit down. (*She sits down on the sofa.*)] We'll find out, young man, we'll find out. But why be ashamed? I've known for a long time that you're not exactly a model of chastity.
PLATONOV: Please, don't ask me any questions, Anna. I don't feel like being present at my own inquest today. [Speak, if you wish, but do not ask me about it.
ANNA: Very well. Did you get my letters?
PLATONOV: Yes.
ANNA: Why, then, didn't you come?
PLATONOV: I can't.
ANNA: Why can't you?
PLATONOV: I'm sorry, I can't.
ANNA: Sulking?
PLATONOV: Good Lord, no. Why should I sulk? Don't ask me, for God's sake.
ANNA: Be so good as to answer my question, Michael. Sit down properly. Why haven't you been to see us these past three weeks?
PLATONOV: I've been sick.
ANNA: You're lying!

PLATONOV: Yes, I'm lying. But, please don't ask me why, Anna.]
ANNA: You simply reek of vodka! What does it all mean, Platonov? What's the matter with you? You look like nothing on earth. Bloodshot eyes, horrible face . . . You're filthy, your rooms are filthy. Take a good look round! It's disgraceful! What is the matter with you? Been drinking?
PLATONOV: Yes.
ANNA: I see. Last year's business all over again. Last year you seduced some girl and the whole summer you went about looking miserable. The same thing's happening now. Don Juan and a pitiful coward rolled into one. Don't you dare drink!
PLATONOV: I won't.
ANNA: Promise? Still, why burden you with promises? (*She gets up.*) Where's your liquor? (Platonov *points to the cupboard.*) [You ought to be ashamed, Michael, to be so cowardly! Where's your strength of character? (*She opens the cupboard.*)] Heavens, what a mess! You'll catch it from Sasha when she comes back. Do you want your wife to come back?
PLATONOV: All I want is that you should ask me no questions and shouldn't look me straight in the eye.
ANNA: Which bottle has vodka in it?
PLATONOV: All of 'em.
ANNA: All five? [You're a real drunkard, aren't you? Why, your cupboard's a regular bar.] It's certainly high time Sasha came back. You'll have to invent some good excuse for her. I'm not really a rival to fear. I'm always ready to come to terms. It isn't my intention to come between you. (*She takes a sip from a bottle.*) Not bad. Come, let's have a little drink. Shall we? Just one and we won't drink any more. (Platonov *goes to the cupboard.*) Hold the glass. (*She pours out the vodka.*) Cheers! [I shan't give you any more.] (Platonov *drinks.*) Now I'll have one too. (*She pours herself out a glass.*) Here's to all bad men! (*She drinks.*) You're one of them! Excellent vodka. You have good taste. (*She hands him the bottles.*) [Take 'em and bring 'em here.

(*They go to the window.*) Now say good-bye to your delicious vodka! (*She looks out of the window.*)] A pity to throw it away, though. Shall we have another? What do you say? Shall we?

PLATONOV: As you like . . .

ANNA (*pours out a drink*): Drink! Quickly.

PLATONOV (*drinks*): Your health! I wish you every happiness.

ANNA (*pours herself out a glass and drinks*): Did you miss me? Let's sit down. Put down the bottle for the time being. (*They sit down.*) Did you miss me?

PLATONOV: Every moment.

ANNA: Why didn't you come then?

PLATONOV: Don't ask me. I won't tell you anything, not because I don't want to be frank with you, but because I don't want to hurt you. My dear, I'm lost. I am done for! Remorse, despondency, depression—in short, torture! You came and at once I began to feel better.

ANNA: You've grown thin. You don't look so handsome any more. Can't stand these romantic heroes. What the hell are you doing to yourself, Platonov? [Acting the hero of some novel? Which novel is it? Depression, despondency, the war of passions, love with footnotes . . . Goodness gracious me!] Can't you behave like a man? Live, foolish man, just as other people live. What do you think you are? An archangel? Why can't you live, breathe, sit like any ordinary mortal?

PLATONOV: It's easy to say that, but what am I to do?

[ANNA: A man lives and doesn't know what to do! That certainly is strange! What are you to do? Very well, let me answer your question as well as I can, though such an idle question doesn't really require an answer.

PLATONOV: You can't answer it.]

ANNA: Well, to begin with, live like a human being. That is to say, don't drink, don't lie about all day long, wash yourself more often and—come to see me. Secondly, be content with what you have. You're playing the fool, my dear sir. Isn't your schoolmastering enough for you? (*She gets up.*) Come home with me now.

PLATONOV: What do you mean? (*He gets up.*) Go to your house? Oh, no!

ANNA: [Come on! You'll see people, you'll talk, you'll listen, you'll get into an argument...

PLATONOV: No, no. Don't ask me.

ANNA: Why not?

PLATONOV: I can't, that's all.

ANNA: Of course, you can. Put on your hat! Come along!

PLATONOV: I can't, Anna. Not for anything in the world. Not a step out of this house.

ANNA: Of course, you can! (*She puts his hat on his head.*) You're playing the fool, my dear Platonov. Don't try to be funny with me. (*She takes him by the arm.*) Well? Left, right! Come on, Platonov! Forward!] (*Pause.*) Why, what's the matter, Michael? Come along!

PLATONOV: I can't.

ANNA: Stubborn as a mule! (*Pause.*) [Start walking. Well? Left, right! Darling Michael, sweet Michael, dearest...

PLATONOV (*tearing himself away*): I'm not coming, Anna.

ANNA: Well, let's go for a walk round the school then.

PLATONOV: Why are you pestering me? I've told you I won't go, haven't I? I want to stay here. So please let me do as I like. (*Pause.*) I won't go.

ANNA: I see.] Look here, Platonov. I'll borrow some money for you and you can go away somewhere for a month or two.

PLATONOV: Where?

ANNA: Moscow, St. Petersburg... Do that, Michael. You want a change badly. Have a nice trip, see people, go to the theatre. You'll feel much better. I'll give you money, letters... Would you like me to come with you? Would you? We'd have a lovely time together. You'll come back here refreshed, radiant.

PLATONOV: It's a delightful idea, but unfortunately it can't be done. I shall be leaving here tomorrow, but not with you.
ANNA: As you wish. Where are you going?
PLATONOV: I'm going . . . (*Pause.*) I'm leaving this place for good.
ANNA: Nonsense! (*She drinks from the bottle.*) Rubbish!
PLATONOV: It isn't nonsense, my dear. I'm going away for good.
ANNA: But why, you funny man?
PLATONOV: Don't ask me. I shall never come back. I'm going and . . . Good-bye! [Don't ask any questions. You won't find anything out from me now.]
ANNA: Rubbish!
PLATONOV: This is the last time we shall be seeing each other. I'll disappear for good . . . (*He takes her by the sleeve, then by the shoulder.*) Forget the fool, the donkey, the scoundrel, the blackguard Platonov. He'll disappear from the face of the earth. He'll efface himself completely. We may perhaps meet again many, many years hence, when both of us will be able to laugh and shed senile tears over these days, but now—oh, to hell with it! (*He kisses her hand.*)
ANNA: Here, have a drink. (*She pours out a glass for him.*) There's no reason why a drunkard should not talk a lot of nonsense, is there?
PLATONOV (*drinks*): I'm not going to get drunk. I shall remember you, my fairy godmother! I shall never forget you! Laugh, clear-headed, intelligent woman! Tomorrow I'm running away from here. I'm running away from myself. Don't know where. Running away to a new life. I've a good idea what that new life will be like!
ANNA: All this is excellent, but what's come over you?
PLATONOV: What's come over me? I . . . You'll find out everything later. My friend, when you're horrified with what I'm about to do, please, do not blame me. Remember that I'm punished already. To part from you for ever is punishment enough. What are you smiling at? You must believe me. Believe me, I

say. I feel so bitter, so bad, so vile that I could strangle myself!

ANNA (*through tears*): I can't believe that you're capable of doing anything horrible. Will you write to me at least?

PLATONOV: I shan't dare to write to you, and you won't want to read my letters. I tell you, I'm going away for good. Good-bye.

[ANNA: I see. You'll be lost without me, Platonov. (*Rubbing her forehead*.) I'm a little drunk. Let's go away together.

PLATONOV: No. Tomorrow you'll find out about everything. (*He turns away to the window*.)

ANNA: Do you need any money?

PLATONOV: No.

ANNA: Are you sure I can't be of any help?

PLATONOV: I don't know. Please send me your photograph today. (*Turning back to her*.) Go away, Anna, or goodness only knows what I may do. I'll burst out sobbing, I'll hurt myself . . . I'll . . . Go away. I can't possibly stay. I'm telling you plainly. What are you waiting for? Please, understand, I have to go away. What are you looking at me like that for? Why pull such a face?

ANNA: Good-bye. (*She gives him her hand*.) We shall see each other again.

PLATONOV: No, we shan't. (*He kisses her hand*.) Good-bye.] Please, leave me. (*He covers his face with her hand*.)

ANNA: The poor boy has gone all soft and sentimental. Well? Let go my hand. Good-bye. Shall we have another drink before we part? (*She pours out the drinks*.) [Drink! Happy journey and happiness at the end of it. (Platonov *drinks*.) I wish you'd stay, Platonov! Won't you? (*She pours out a drink for herself and drinks it*.) We'd have a lovely time together. What sort of crime is this? Is it possible in Voynitsevka? (*Pause*.) Have another one to drown your sorrows?

PLATONOV: Why not?

ANNA (*she pours him out a drink*): Drink, darling. Oh, damn it all!

PLATONOV (*drinks*): I hope you'll be happy. Go on living here. You don't want me.]

ANNA: If we're going to drink, we may as well drink properly. (*She pours out a drink.*) If you drink you die, and if you don't drink you die, so why not drink and die? (*She drinks.*) I'm a drunkard, Platonov. Shall I pour you out another glass? Well, perhaps not. It will make us tongue-tied, and we shan't be able to talk. (*She sits down.*) There's nothing worse than an educated woman who has nothing to do. What use am I? What do I live for? (*Pause.*) I can't help being immoral. I'm an immoral woman, Platonov. Don't you think so? Maybe I love you because I'm an immoral woman. (*Rubbing her forehead.*) I'm quite sure to make a mess of my life. Women like me always do. I should have been a headmistress or a professor. If I'd been a diplomat, I'd have set the whole world by the ears. An educated woman—with nothing to do ... Why, that means that I'm not wanted. Horses, cows, and dogs are wanted, but I'm not—I am redundant. What do you think? Why don't you say something?

PLATONOV: We're in a hell of a mess, you and I, aren't we?

ANNA: If only I had children. Are you fond of children? (*She gets up.*) Please, stay, darling. Will you? [We'd have such a lovely time together. Happy, no quarrelling.] If you go away, what's going to happen to me? [I want to have a rest, don't I? Michael, I must have a rest. I want to be—a wife, a mother.] (*Pause.*) Why are you silent? Say something! Are you going to stay? You—you do love me, don't you, you funny fellow. You do, don't you?

PLATONOV (*looking out of the window*): I shall kill myself if I stay.

ANNA: You do love me, don't you?

PLATONOV: Who doesn't love you?

ANNA: You love me and I love you, what more do you want! [You must be going off your head. What more do you want?] Why didn't you come to me that night? (*Pause.*) Will you stay?

PLATONOV: Go away, for God's sake! You're torturing me.

ANNA (*giving him her hand*): Very well, in that case ... good luck!

PLATONOV: [Go away or I'll tell you everything. If I do that, I'll kill myself.

ANNA: I'm giving you my hand. Can't you see? I'll come to see you for a minute in the evening.

PLATONOV: Don't! I'll come to say good-bye to you myself. I'll come I promise you ... No, I won't come.] You'll never see me again and I won't see you again. You won't want to see me yourself. You won't want to have anything to do with me ever. A new life. (*He embraces and kisses her.*) For the last time. (*He pushes her through the door.*) Good-bye. Go and—good luck. (*He bolts the door.*)

ANNA (*behind the door*): I swear we will see each other again!

PLATONOV: Never! Good-bye! [(*He stops his ears.*) I can't hear anything. Shut up and go away. I've stopped up my ears.]

ANNA: I'm going. I'll send Sergey to you and I promise you you won't leave. If you do, you'll leave with me. Good-bye. (*Pause.*)

PLATONOV: Has she gone? (*He goes up to the door and listens.*) She's gone. Perhaps not? (*He opens the door.*) A real demon of a woman ... (*He looks out through the door.*) Gone. (*He lies down on the sofa.*) Good-bye, my dear! (*He sighs.*) I'll never see her again ... [She's gone. I wish she had stayed another five minutes. (*Pause.*) Not at all a bad idea. I'll ask Sophia to put off our departure for two weeks or so and go off with Anna. Only for two weeks! She couldn't object to that, could she? I'm sure she'll agree. She can stay with her mother for the time being. Shall I ask her? Shall I? While I'm away with Anna, Sophia can have a rest. I mean, recover her strength. After all, I wouldn't be going away for ever. (*There's a knock at the door.*) I'll go. It's settled. Excellent!] (*There is another knock.*) Who is it? You, Anna? Who's there? (*Another knock.*) Is it you? (*He gets up.*) I won't let you in. (*He goes to the door.*) Anna? (*Another knock.*) I believe she's giggling. (*He laughs.*) It is her! I must have a look. (*Opens the door.*) Good Lord! (*Enter Osip.*) What's all this? What has brought you here, you devil?

OSIP: How are you, sir?

PLATONOV: What have you got to tell me? To what and to whom do I owe the honour of a visit from such an important personage? Tell me quickly and get the hell out of here.

OSIP: I think I'll sit down, sir. (*He sits down.*)

PLATONOV: Please do. (*Pause.*) What's happened to you, Osip? What's the matter with you? All the ten Egyptian plagues are written on your face. What's been happening to you? You're pale, thin, haggard. Are you ill?

OSIP: The same plagues are written on your face too, sir. What's been happening to you? The devil is chasing me, but what about you?

PLATONOV: Me? I'm not acquainted with the devil. I am chasing myself. (*Touching* Osip *on the shoulder.*) Skin and bones.

OSIP: And where's your fat gone, sir? Are you ill, sir? Ill from good behaviour?

PLATONOV (*sits down beside him*): Why have you come?

OSIP: I've come to say good-bye, sir.

PLATONOV: Oh? Are you going away?

OSIP: No, sir, I'm not going away. You're going away.

PLATONOV: I see! How do you know?

OSIP: I know it all right.

PLATONOV: I'm not going away, my dear fellow. You're wasting your time.

OSIP: You are going away, sir.

PLATONOV: You know everything and everything seems to be your business. You're a magician, Osip. I am going away, my dear fellow. You're quite right.

OSIP: There you are! I know, you see. I even know where you're going, sir.

PLATONOV: Oh? You certainly are a marvel. You see, I don't know it myself. You're a sage, a perfect sage. Well, tell me, where am I going?

OSIP: Do you really want to know, sir?

PLATONOV: Good heavens, man, I'm interested. Where?
OSIP: To the next world, sir.
PLATONOV: It's a long way! (*Pause.*) A mystery. Are you going to send me there?
OSIP: Yes, sir. I've brought you your ticket.
PLATONOV: Very nice of you. So you've come to kill me, have you?
OSIP: Yes, sir.
PLATONOV (*mimicking him*): Yes, sir. What an impudent fellow, damn him! Came to send me to the next world, if you please! Are you going to kill me of your own free will or has someone commissioned you to do it?
OSIP (*showing him a twenty-five rouble note*): Here. Vengerovich gave me this money to cripple your lordship. (*He tears up the note.*)
PLATONOV: Aha! Old Vengerovich?
OSIP: Yes, sir.
PLATONOV: Why then did you tear up the money? Want to show how magnanimous you are?
OSIP: No, sir. I tore up the note so that in the next world you shouldn't think that I killed you for money. (Platonov *gets up and starts walking up and down the stage.*) Are you afraid, sir? Scared? (*He laughs.*) Run, shout! I'm not stopping you: you can go if you like. Go and call for help. Tell them Osip has come to kill you. So he has. You don't believe me, sir? (*Pause.*)
PLATONOV (*walks up to* Osip *and looks at him*): Amazing! (*Pause.*) What are you smiling at? Fool! (*Strikes him on the arm.*) Don't you dare smile. I'm talking to you! Silence! I'll see that you hang. I'll tear you limb from limb, you brigand! (*He moves quickly away from* Osip.) However ... Don't make me angry. I mustn't be made angry. It gives me a pain ...
OSIP: Please, slap my face, sir, for being a bad man.
PLATONOV: By all means. (*He goes up to* Osip *and slaps his face.*) Well? Reeling? You wait! You'll be reeling all right when a

154

hundred sticks are striking your empty head. Remember how pock-marked Filka died?

OSIP: To a cur—a cur's death, sir.

PLATONOV: Oh, how disgusting you are, you rat! Why do you go on hurting people like some plague, some gangrene? What have they done to you? Oh, you blackguard! (*He slaps his face again and again.*) You horror! I'll show you! I'll ... (*He moves away quickly.*) Get out of here!

OSIP: Spit in my eye, sir, because I'm a bad man.

PLATONOV: I wouldn't waste my spittle on you!

OSIP (*getting up*): And you dare talk like this to me, sir?

PLATONOV: Get out before I trample on you!

OSIP: You wouldn't dare. You're also a bad man, sir.

PLATONOV: Talking to me are you? (*He goes up to him.*) You came to kill me, I believe. All right, kill me! Here I am. Come on, kill me!

OSIP: I used to respect you, Mr. Platonov. I used to think you were a big man. But now . . . [Why, I wouldn't lay a hand on you, but, I'm afraid,] I have to kill you. You're too harmful to live. Why did the young lady come to see you today?

PLATONOV (*shaking him by the chest*): Kill me! Come on, kill me!

OSIP: And why did the general's lady come after her? You're deceiving her, too, aren't you? And where's your wife? Which of the three of them is the woman you really care for? Do you still say you're not a bad man? (*He quickly trips him up. They fall together to the floor.*)

PLATONOV: I'll kill you first! I'm stronger than you. (*They struggle.*) Don't make such a confounded noise.

OSIP: Lie on your stomach! Don't twist my arm! My arm has done nothing to you, so why twist it? No, you don't! Give my humble regards to General Voynitsev when you meet him in the next world.

PLATONOV: Let go!

OSIP (*taking a knife out of his belt*): Keep still! I'm going to kill you all the same. Strong, aren't you? A big man! You don't want to die, do you? You didn't ought to have touched what don't belong to you!

PLATONOV (*shouts*): My arm! Wait, wait! My arm!

OSIP: So you don't want to die, do you, sir? You'll be in the Kingdom of Heaven in no time.

PLATONOV: Don't strike me in the back! Not in the back, you animal! Strike me in the chest. My arm! Let go, Osip! I have a wife, a son! How your knife flashes! (Sasha *runs in.*)

SASHA: What's the matter? (*She screams.*) Michael! (*She runs to the struggling men and falls on top of them.*) What are you doing!

OSIP: Who's that? You, ma'am? (*He jumps up.*) I'll let him live. (*To* Sasha.) Here's my knife. Take it. (*He gives her the knife.*) I shan't cut his throat in front of you. I'll cut his throat later. He won't escape! (*He jumps out through the window.*)

PLATONOV (*after a pause*): The devil! Hullo, Sasha! (*He groans.*)

SASHA: He hasn't injured you, has he? Can you stand up? Quick!

PLATONOV: I don't know. The dirty swine! He's made of iron. Give me your hand. (*He gets up.*) Don't be frightened, my dear. I'm safe and sound. He only crushed me a little.

SASHA: What a scoundrel! I told you not to have anything to do with him.

PLATONOV: Where's the sofa? What are you looking at me like that for? Your unfaithful husband is still alive. Can't you see? (*He lies down on the sofa.*) Thanks for coming or you would have been a widow and I a dead man.

SASHA: Lie down on this pillow. (*She puts a pillow under his head.*) So! (*She sits down at his feet.*) You're sure it doesn't hurt anywhere? (*Pause.*) Why have you closed your eyes?

PLATONOV: No, no. I just felt like it. You've come, Sasha? My treasure has come back to me. (*He kisses her hand.*)

SASHA: Little Nicholas is ill.

PLATONOV: What's the matter with him?

SASHA: He has a bad cough, a high temperature, a rash. He hasn't slept for two nights and he's been crying all the time. He won't eat, he won't drink. (*She cries.*) He's seriously ill, Michael. I'm terribly afraid for him. And I've had a bad dream too.

PLATONOV: What's your dear brother doing? He's a doctor, isn't he?

SASHA: You can't expect him to show any sympathy! He came to see us four days ago, stayed a few minutes and went away. I tell him about little Nicholas's illness, but he just yawns.

PLATONOV: Another stupid fool! He'll miss himself one day. Run away from himself when he falls ill.

SASHA: What shall I do?

[PLATONOV: Hope for the best! Are you living at your father's now?

SASHA: Yes.

PLATONOV: How is he?

SASHA: He's all right. Walks up and down the room, smokes his pipe, and promises to come and see you. I looked very worried when I arrived at his house. Well, so he guessed that I . . . that you and I . . . what am I going to do about Nicholas?]

PLATONOV: Don't worry, Sasha.

SASHA: How can I help worrying? What if he dies, God forbid? What will happen to us then?

PLATONOV: God won't take away our little boy from you. Why should he punish you unless it is for marrying a good-for-nothing like me? (*Pause.*) Take care of our little boy, Sasha. [Take care of him for me and I swear to you by all that's holy that I'll make a man of him. Every step he takes will make you happy. Poor little fellow, he, too, is a Platonov. He ought to change his name. As a man I'm insignificant and small, but as a father I shall be great. Don't be afraid for his future. Oh, my arm!] (*He groans.*) My arm aches. That brigand bruised it badly. What's the matter with it? (*Examining his arm.*) It's red. Oh, to hell with it! So that's how it is, Sasha. You'll be happy with your son! [You're laughing! Laugh, my treasure. Now you're crying. What are you crying for? I see . . . Don't cry, Sasha. (*He kisses her head*.) You've come back. Why did you go away?] Don't cry, darling! Why all these tears? I love you, my little one. I love you very much. It's all my fault, but it can't be helped can it? You must forgive me. There, there.

SASHA: Is that affair of yours over?

PLATONOV: Affair? What a word to use, you little chump!

SASHA: So it isn't over, is it?

PLATONOV: What can I say to you? There has never been any affair. It's just a kind of stupendous absurdity. [Don't be too worried by this nonsense.] If it isn't over yet, it'll be over soon.

SASHA: But when?

PLATONOV: Very soon, I should think. [We shall soon live again as before, Sasha. To hell with all this—new life! I'm worn out. I'm played out. Don't worry, it's not going to last, this affair.] I'm sure it won't last. It's not serious. She'll be the first to cool off. She'll be the first to laugh at it, to be sorry it has happened. [Sophia is no match for me. She still believes in ideas I've ceased to believe in long ago. She's moved to tears by things that make me laugh. She's no match for me. (*Pause*.)] Believe me, Sophia will not be your rival much longer. Sasha, what's the matter?

SASHA *gets up and sways*.

PLATONOV (*rising*): Sasha!

SASHA: It's—it's Sophia and not Anna?

PLATONOV: Is this the first time you've heard of it?

SASHA: Sophia! Why, it's contemptible! It's vile!

[PLATONOV: What's the matter with you? You're pale. You're swaying. (*He groans*.) At least you mustn't torment me, Sasha. My arm aches, and now you . . . Is it really news to you? Is this the first you've heard of it? Why then did you leave me that night? Not because of Sophia?]

SASHA: With Anna it wouldn't have mattered so much. But with someone else's wife! I didn't expect such a mean, such a sinful action from you. God will punish you for it, you shameless man! (*She goes towards the door.*)

PLATONOV (*after a pause*): Shocked, are you? Where are you going?

[SASHA (*stops at the door*): God grant you happiness.

PLATONOV: Whom?

SASHA: Sophia and you.

PLATONOV: You've read too many silly novels, Sasha. I'm still your husband. We've got a son. And, anyway, it's not happiness I want.] Don't leave me, Sasha! [You're going away. I suppose this time it is forever, isn't it?

SASHA: I can't . . . Oh, my God, my God!

PLATONOV: You can't?

SASHA: My God, can this be true? (*She puts her hand to her temples and squats down on the floor.*) I—I don't know what to do.

PLATONOV: You don't? (*He goes up to her.*) Well, it's for you to decide. I wish you'd stay with me, though.] Why are you crying, you silly little darling? (*Pause.*) Oh, Sasha, Sasha! I've treated you badly, but can't you really forgive me?

SASHA: Have you forgiven yourself?

PLATONOV: A philosophical question. (*He kisses her on the head.*) I told you I was sorry. Don't you see that without you it would be vodka, filth, Osip . . . I'm worn out. Stay with me as a nurse, if not as a wife. [What strange people you women are! You, too, Sasha, are strange.] If you feed that scoundrel Osip, if you can't tear yourself away from your cats and dogs, if you sit up till midnight saying prayers for some supposed enemies of yours, why can't you throw a crust to your guilty, repentant husband? Why do you, too, come to me as my executioner? Stay, Sasha. (*He embraces her.*) I can't manage without a nurse. I'm a scoundrel. I took away the wife of my friend, I'm Sophia's lover, [perhaps even Anna's lover, too. I'm a polygamist. A great rogue from the point of view of a family as an institution.]

Be shocked, be indignant. But who'll love you as much as I do? Who'll respect you so highly as I do darling? Who will you cook dinner for? Whose soup will you put too much salt in? You'll be quite justified in leaving me. Justice demands it, but —(*he lifts her up*) who'll pick you up like this? Are you sure you'll be able to live without me, my treasure?

SASHA: I can't. Let me go. I'm done for. You're joking while I'm suffering. (*She tears herself away from him.*) Don't you realize that it's no joke? Good-bye! I can't live with you! Now everyone will think you a despicable man. How do you think that will make me feel? (*She sobs.*)

PLATONOV: All right, go! (*He kisses her on the head and lies down on the sofa.*) I understand . . .

SASHA: You've destroyed our family. We lived so happily, so contentedly. There was no one in the world happier than me. (*She sits down.*) What have you done, Michael? You can't undo it now . . . I'm done for. (*She sobs.*)

PLATONOV: Go, for heaven's sake!

SASHA: Good-bye! You won't see me again! Don't come to see us. Father will bring Nicholas to see you. May God forgive you, as I forgive you. You've ruined our life!

PLATONOV: Haven't you gone yet?

SASHA: I'm going. All right . . . (*She gazes for some time at* Platonov *and goes out.*)

PLATONOV: And this is the man for whom a new life begins? Good Lord, Sasha, a little fly like her, and she, too, thinks she has a right to throw stones at me on the strength of some kind of religious scruples. What a damnable situation! (*He lies down on the sofa.* Voynitsev *enters and stops at the door. After a pause.*) Is this the epilogue or is the comedy still continuing? (*Seeing* Voynitsev, *he closes his eyes and begins to snore slightly.*)

VOYNITSEV (*going up to* Platonov): Platonov! (*Pause.*) You're not asleep. I can see it by your face. (*He sits down beside him.*) I don't think this is quite the occasion for a quiet nap. (Platonov *gets up.* Voynitsev *gets up and looks out of the window.*) [You've killed me. Do you realize that? (*Pause.*) Thank you . . . Do you realize what you've done to me? I suppose you couldn't help it. It seems this is how it had to be . . . (*He weeps.* Platonov *gets up and walks slowly towards the other corner of the room.*) For once in my life I got a present from Fate and—even that has been taken away!] Not satisfied with being intelligent, attractive, magnanimous, you had to have my happiness too! You've taken it away from me, and I—what about me? I don't count. It was bound to happen. I'm not too clever, I'm sentimental, effeminate . . . With a disposition to idleness and mysticism . . . I'm superstitious . . . You have delivered the *coup de grâce*, friend!

PLATONOV: Go away, there's a good fellow!

VOYNITSEV: Presently . . . I was coming to challenge you to a duel, and now that I've come all I can do is cry. I'm going. (*Pause.*) Have I lost her for good?

PLATONOV: Yes.

VOYNITSEV (*whistles*): I see. Well, of course.

PLATONOV: Go away, please! I beg you, go away!

VOYNITSEV: Presently. I've nothing to do here, have I? (*He goes towards the door.*) No, there's nothing I can do here now. (*Pause.*) Give her back to me, Platonov! Be good! She is mine, Platonov! You're happy as it is. Save me, my dear fellow. Give her back to me. (*He bursts out sobbing.*) She's mine, mine! Understand?

PLATONOV (*going back to the sofa*): Go away! I'll shoot myself. I swear I will.

VOYNITSEV: Don't . . . Never mind. (*He waves his hand and goes out.*)

PLATONOV (*clutching his head*): Unhappy, miserable wretch! Oh, my God! [To hell with that head of mine, which even God seems to have abandoned! (*He sobs.*) Don't go near people, you loathsome creature!] I've brought misfortune to people and they've brought misfortune to me. Keep away from people! They strike at me, but they don't strike me down. Under every chair, under every chip of wood, there sits a murderer, looking into my eyes, trying to kill me! Strike me! (*Striking his breast.*) Kill me, before I kill myself! (*Running to the door.*) Don't strike at my breast! My breast is already torn to pieces! (*He shouts.*) Sasha! Sasha! For God's sake! (*He opens the door.* Glagolyev Sr. *enters, muffled up, and leaning on a crutch.*)

GLAGOLYEV SR.: Are you at home, Platonov? I'm so glad. I'm not disturbing you, am I? I shan't detain you. I shall be leaving presently. I want to ask you one question. Give me your answer and I'll go. What's the matter, my dear fellow? You look pale, you're swaying, you're trembling . . . What's the matter with you?

PLATONOV: What's the matter with me? Well, I expect I must be drunk or—going mad. I'm drunk—drunk! My head's spinning . . .

GLAGOLYEV SR. (*aside*): I'll ask him. What soberness conceals drunkenness reveals. (*To* Platonov.) My question may seem strange to you, even stupid, perhaps, but, for God's sake, give me your answer, Platonov. The question is of vital importance to me. I shall believe your answer because I know you to be a most honest man. Let my question appear strange, absurd, stupid, and perhaps even insulting to you, but, for God's sake —answer it! I find myself in a most terrible position. Our mutual friend . . . you know her well . . . I considered her the model of perfection, I mean, Anna Voynitsev. (*He supports* Platonov.) Don't fall, for goodness sake.

PLATONOV: Go away! I always thought you were a—stupid old man!

GLAGOLYEV SR.: You're her friend. You know her well . . . People have either slandered her to me or—opened my eyes. Is she an honest woman, Platonov? Is she? Is she? has she the right to become the wife of an honourable man? (*Pause.*) I don't know how to formulate my question. Please, try to understand me. I was told that she . . .

PLATONOV: Everything in this world is vile, contemptible, filthy! Everything—vile, contemptible . . . (*He faints and falls against* Glagolyev Sr. *and collapses in a heap on the floor.*)

GLAGOLYEV JR. (*entering*): You've been a long time here, haven't you? I'm not going to wait any longer!

GLAGOLYEV SR.: Everything is vile, filthy, contemptible—including her too, I suppose.

GLAGOLYEV JR. (*looking at* Platonov): What's the matter with Platonov, father?

GLAGOLYEV SR.: He's disgustingly drunk. Yes, vile, filthy! A profound, merciless, stinging truth! (*Pause.*) We're leaving for Paris.

GLAGOLYEV JR.: What did you say? Pa . . . Pa . . . Paris? What are *you* going to do in Paris? (*Bursts out laughing.*)

GLAGOLYEV SR.: To wallow in filth, just as this one's wallowing. (*Points to* Platonov.)

GLAGOLYEV JR.: Wallow? In—Paris?

GLAGOLYEV SR.: Let's go and look for happiness somewhere else. Enough! It's high time I stopped performing a comedy for my own benefit, going on fooling myself with ideals! There's no more faith, no more love! There are no more human beings! Let's go!

GLAGOLYEV JR.: To Paris?

GLAGOLYEV SR.: Yes. If we're going to sin, let's sin in a foreign country rather than in our own. Be my teacher, son! To Paris!

GLAGOLYEV JR.: Now, that *is* nice, father. You taught me to read and I'll teach you to live! Let's go! (*They go out.*)

END OF ACT THREE

ACT FOUR

The study of the late General Voynitsev. Two doors, old-fashioned furniture, Persian rugs, flowers. The walls are hung with rifles, pistols, daggers (of Caucasian workmanship), etc. Family portraits. Busts of Krylov, Pushkin and Gogol. A glass cabinet with stuffed birds. A bookcase. On the bookcase cigarette holders, boxes, sticks, rifle barrels, etc. A writing desk piled high with papers, portraits, statuettes and firearms. It is morning.

[SOPHIA *and* KATYA *come in.*

SOPHIA: Don't be so excited. Talk sensibly.

KATYA: Something awful is happening, madam. The doors and windows of the schoolhouse are wide open, everything is turned upside down in the rooms, the furniture's broken ... The door has been torn off its hinges. Something awful must have happened there. It wasn't for nothing that one of our hens started crowing like a cock.

SOPHIA: What do you think happened?

KATYA: I'm sure I don't know, ma'am. All I know is that something awful must have happened. Either Mr. Platonov has gone away for good or he's committed suicide. He's very hot tempered, he is, ma'am. I've known him for two years, ma'am.

SOPHIA: No, I don't think so. Have you been down to the village, Katya?

KATYA: Yes, ma'am. He's nowhere to be found. I went about looking for him for four hours, ma'am.

SOPHIA (*sitting down*): What am I to do? What can I do? (*Pause.*) Are you quite sure he's nowhere to be found? Are you sure?

KATYA: I don't know, ma'am. I'm sure something awful must have happened. It's not for nothing that I have such a gnawing pain in my heart. Give him up, ma'am. It's a sin. (*She weeps.*) I'm sorry for the young master, ma'am. Such a handsome man and look at him now! He's worried himself to death, poor gentleman. Walks about in a daze. He was such a good master and now he's gone all to pieces. I'm sorry for Mr. Platonov, too, ma'am. He used to be such a gay gentleman. He made you feel so cheerful. And now he looks more dead than alive. Do give it up, ma'am.

SOPHIA: Give what up?

KATYA: This love affair, ma'am. What's the sense of it? Oh, the shame of it! I'm sorry for you, too, ma'am. You look awful! You've grown thin, you don't eat, you don't drink, you don't sleep, all you do is cough.

SOPHIA: Go and look for him again, Katya. Perhaps he is back at the school.

KATYA: Yes'm. (*Pause.*) You really ought to go to bed, ma'am.

SOPHIA: Go there again, Katya. Haven't you gone yet?

KATYA (*aside*): You're not as strong as a peasant girl. (*In a sharp, whining voice.*) Where am I to go, ma'am?

SOPHIA: I'm so sleepy. Haven't slept all night. Don't shout so loudly! Go away!

KATYA: Very good, ma'am. You shouldn't take it so much to heart, ma'am. You'd better go to your room and lie down. (*She goes out.*)]

SOPHIA: This is awful! He gave me his word of honour yesterday to be at the hut at ten o'clock and he didn't come. I waited for him till daybreak . . . His word of honour! Is that love? Is that the way we were going to leave? He doesn't love me!

VOYNITSEV (*entering*): [I'd better lie down. Perhaps I'll fall asleep somehow. (*Catching sight of* Sophia.)] You—here? In my study?

SOPHIA: Me—here? (*Looking round.*) Yes. I must have come in here by mistake, without noticing . . . (*She goes to the door.*)

VOYNITSEV: One moment!

SOPHIA (*stopping*): Well?

VOYNITSEV: [Please let me have two or three minutes. Can you stay here for two or three minutes?

SOPHIA: Did you want to say something? Say it.

VOYNITSEV: Yes . . . (*Pause.*) There was a time when you and I were not strangers in this room.

SOPHIA: Yes, there was.

VOYNITSEV: I'm sorry. I don't think I know what I'm talking about.] Are you going away?

SOPHIA: Yes.

VOYNITSEV: I see. Soon?

SOPHIA: Today.

VOYNITSEV: With him?

SOPHIA: Yes.

VOYNITSEV: I hope you'll be happy. (*Pause.*) Good material for happiness! Carnal lust and the misfortune of another. The misfortune of another is always somebody else's good fortune. However, this isn't original, is it? [People listen more willingly to a new lie than an old truth. Oh, well, never mind! Live as you know best.]

SOPHIA: I believe you wanted to say something.

VOYNITSEV: Why? Haven't I been saying something? All right. This is what I wanted to say. I want to be absolutely fair to you. I don't want to owe you anything. That's why I'd like to apologize to you for my behaviour last night. I said a lot of things I shouldn't have said to you. I was rude and spiteful. I'm sorry. Do you forgive me?

SOPHIA: I forgive you. (*She is about to go out.*)

VOYNITSEV: Wait, wait! That's not all! I've something more to say. (*Sighing.*) [I'm going mad, Sophy. I haven't the strength to recover from this terrible blow. I'm going mad, but I'm still able to understand everything. In my head, enveloped in a thick fog, in a kind of grey, leaden, heavy fog, there's still a bright spot which makes it possible for me to understand things. If this spot too disappears, I'm completely done for I understand everything. (*Pause.*) I'm standing in my study. It used to be the study of my father, Major-General Voynitsev, of the suite of His Majesty, holder of the Order of St. George, a great and famous man. People only saw the stains on him. They only saw how he beat and trampled on people, but how he was beaten and trampled on no one cared to see. (*Pointing to* Sophia.) This is my ex-wife. (Sophia *turns to go*.) Wait! Let me finish. I may be talking foolishly, but, please, listen to me! For the last time!]

SOPHIA: You've said everything already. What more can you say? [We must part. What else is there to say?] Do you want to prove that I am to blame? Don't bother! I know what to think of myself.

VOYNITSEV: What can I say? Oh, Sophy, Sophy! You know nothing. Nothing or you wouldn't look at me with such disdain. You'd be horrified if you knew what was going on inside me! (*He kneels before her.*) What are you doing, Sophy? [Where are you pushing yourself and me? For God's sake, have pity! I'm dying! I'm going mad! Don't leave me! I'll forget everything. I've already forgiven everything. I'll be your slave. I'll love you, I'll love you as I've never loved you before. I'll make you happy. You will be happy as a goddess with me. You'll never be happy with him. You'll only destroy yourself and destroy him. You'll destroy Platonov, Sophy! I know you can't make anyone love you by force, but don't leave me! You'll be gay again. You won't be so deathly pale, so unhappy. I'll be a man again and—Platonov will again be coming to see us. It may be just a pipe-dream, but—don't leave me!] Let's bring back the past before it's too late. Platonov will agree. I know him. He doesn't love you. It just happened. You gave yourself to him and he took you. (*Getting up.*) You're crying?

SOPHIA (*getting up*): [Don't think these tears are on your account.] Maybe Platonov will agree. Let him agree. (*Sharply*.) You're mean, despicable, all of you. Where is Platonov?

VOYNITSEV: I don't know.

[SOPHIA: Leave me alone! Don't worry me! I hate you! Go away! Where is Platonov? You're all mean! Where is he? I hate you!

VOYNITSEV: Why?

SOPHIA: Where is he?

VOYNITSEV: I gave him money and he promised to leave. If he carried out his promise, he must have left already.

SOPHIA: You bribed him? Why are you telling lies?

VOYNITSEV: I gave him a thousand roubles and he agreed to give you up. Oh, well, I *am* lying! It's all a lie. Don't believe anything I say, for goodness sake! He's alive and well, your damn Platonov. Go and take him! Kiss him! I did not bribe him, but do you really think that you and he will be happy? And this is my wife? My Sophia? What does it all mean?] I still can't believe it. Your love affair is just platonic, isn't it? It hasn't come to anything—serious, has it?

SOPHIA: I'm his wife, his mistress, anything you like! [(*She turns to go*.) Why are you keeping me here? I've no time to listen to all sorts of . . .]

VOYNITSEV: [Wait, Sophia!] You're his mistress? [Why did you do it?] You speak so boldly. (*He seizes her by the hand*.) How could you do it? How could you? (*Enter* Anna.)

SOPHIA: Leave me alone! (*She goes out*.)

ANNA *goes over to the window and looks out.*

VOYNITSEV (*gesticulating*): It's the end. (*Pause*.) What's happening out there?

ANNA: The peasants have killed Osip.

VOYNITSEV: Already?

ANNA: Yes. Near the well. Do you see? There he is.

VOYNITSEV (*looking out of the window*): Well, serves him right. (*Pause.*)

ANNA: Heard the news, my dear? They say Platonov has disappeared and . . . Have you read the letter?

VOYNITSEV: I have.

ANNA: So it's good-bye to the estate! How do you like that? Gone . . . The Lord gave and the Lord took away. So much for your famous financial conjuring trick! And all because we believed Glagolyev. He promised to buy the estate and never turned up at the auction. His servants say he's gone to Paris. What a joke to play on us in his old age! The dirty swine! But for him we'd have gone on living here and paying the interest on the mortgage quietly, without fuss. (*She sighs.*) Never trust your enemies in this world—nor your friends!

VOYNITSEV: No. One certainly should not trust one's friends.

ANNA: Well, feudal lord? What are you going to do now? Where will you go? God gave it all to your forefathers, but he's taken it away from you. You've nothing left.

VOYNITSEV: It's all the same to me.

ANNA: It isn't all the same. [What are you going to eat? Let's sit down. (*They sit down.*) Don't look so gloomy. You can't do anything about it.] You can't help being sorry to have to say good-bye to your country seat, but what can you do, my dear? There's no way of getting it back. It had to be like that, it seems. Be wise, Sergey. The important thing now is not to give way to despair.

VOYNITSEV: Don't take any notice of me, mother. Why talk about me? You're far from calm yourself. Comfort yourself first, and then come and comfort me.

ANNA: [Well, it's not a question of the women now. In a matter like this the women always remain in the background.] The important thing is not to give way to despair. [You've lost what you've had, and what's important now is not your past but your future.] You've the whole of your life before you, a good hard-working life, a man's life. Why worry? You'll get a job at a prep-school or at a secondary school and you'll start working. I know you won't let me down. You're a philologist, you're not a politically suspect person, you've never been involved in any trouble. You have your convictions, you're a quiet man, you're married. You'll go far if you want to. You're a clever boy. Only you mustn't quarrel with your wife. You've just got married, and already you're quarrelling. Why don't you tell me about it, Sergey? You're unhappy, but you don't say anything. What's happening between you?

VOYNITSEV: It's not happening, it's happened.

ANNA: What has happened? Or is it a secret?

VOYNITSEV (*sighs*): A terrible misfortune has befallen our house, mother. I don't know why I haven't told you about it before. I kept hoping and, besides, I was ashamed to tell you. I only found out about it yesterday morning. I don't care a damn about the estate!

ANNA (*laughing*): You do scare me, I must say. She hasn't been angry with you, has she?

VOYNITSEV: You may well laugh! I'm sure when I tell you you'll have even more reason to laugh. (*Pause.*) She has been unfaithful to me. Let me introduce myself: a cuckold!

ANNA: What nonsense, Sergey! What a ridiculous idea! To say such monstrous things and to talk about them so unthinkingly. You're quite an extraordinary man! Sometimes you blurt something out which makes one sick to listen to you. A cuckold, indeed! You don't know the meaning of the word.

VOYNITSEV: I know, mother. Not in theory, but in practice.

ANNA: Don't insult your wife, you ridiculous man! Oh dear!

VOYNITSEV: I swear to you it's true! (*Pause.*)

ANNA: I don't believe it. You're talking about something that is quite impossible. You're slandering her. It's impossible. Here, in Voynitsevka?

VOYNITSEV: Yes, here, in your damn Voynitsevka.

ANNA: I see. Who in our damned Voynitsevka could have conceived the impossible idea of planting a pair of horns on your aristocratic head? Absolutely no one! Cyril Glagolyev, perhaps, but Glagolyev stopped visiting us. There's no one here who could possibly interest your Sophia. You're just stupidly jealous, my dear.

VOYNITSEV: Platonov!

ANNA: What about Platonov?

VOYNITSEV: It's him!

ANNA (*jumping up*): [One can say all sorts of stupid things, but such stupid things as you've said just . . . blurted out!] This is too much. There's a limit to everything. It's unpardonably stupid!

VOYNITSEV: Ask her, go and ask him, if you don't believe me. I didn't want to believe it myself and I still don't want to believe it. She's going away today. She's leaving me. You can't help believing that, can you? He's going with her. Why, don't you see that I'm going about looking heartbroken and dejected? I'm done for.

ANNA: It can't be, Sergey. You're just letting your childish imagination run away with you. Believe me, nothing of the sort has happened.

VOYNITSEV: I tell you she's leaving today! For the last two days she never stopped telling me that she was his mistress. She herself! What's happened may be impossible to believe, but one has to believe it, whatever one may wish to the contrary.

ANNA: I remember now! I remember . . . I see it all now. Give me a chair, Sergey. No, thank you. So that's what it is! I see it now. Wait, wait! Let me remember it all properly . . . (*Pause. Enter Bugrov.*)

BUGROV: Good morning. How are you all?

ANNA: Yes, yes, yes. This is terrible.

BUGROV: It's raining, but it's hot. (*He mops his brow.*) Phew! Boiling hot, walk or ride. Are you all right, ma'am? (*Pause.*) I've really called because—er—there was the auction yesterday, as you know, and—er—it being a little (*laughs*) painful and a trifle vexing for you, I—er—hope that you won't be offended with me. It wasn't me who bought the estate. Abram Vengerovich bought it. It was only in my name.

VOYNITSEV (*ringing the bell hard*): Damn 'em all! ...

BUGROV: No, ma'am, it wasn't me. It was only in my name, you understand. (*He sits down.*)

YAKOV *enters.*

VOYNITSEV (*to* Yakov): How many times have I told you, scoundrels, blackguards, (*he coughs*) villains, not to let anyone in without announcing them first. You all want a good flogging, you brutes. (*He throws the bell under the table.*) Get out of here! The blackguards! (*He walks up and down the stage. Yakov shrugs and goes out.*)

BUGROV (*coughs*): It was only in my name, ma'am. Abram Vengerovich asked me to tell you that you can go on living here until Christmas, if you like. They'll be making some little alterations here, but they shouldn't be getting in your way. If they do, you can move into the servants' wing. Lots of room there and it's warm. He also told me to ask you, madam, whether you'd like to sell your mines to me—in my name, that is. The mines are yours, ma'am. We'll offer you a good price for them.

ANNA: No, thank you. I damn well won't sell my mines to anyone. What are you going to offer me for them? A few farthings? You know what you can do with them!

BUGROV: Vengerovich also instructed me to tell you, ma'am, that if you refused to sell him your mines and deduct the money Mr. Voynitsev and your late husband owed him, he would present his bills of exchange. I'll present mine as well, ma'am! He, he, he! Friendship, you know, is one thing and money's another. Business is businesss, ma'am! Aye, I'm very sorry, I'm sure. You see, ma'am, I've bought your bills from Petrin.

VOYNITSEV: I shan't allow anyone to count on my bills being paid from my step-mother's estate. It's her estate, not mine.
BUGROV: I dare say your mother will take pity on you, sir.
VOYNITSEV: I haven't any time to talk to you. I don't care! (*He gestures with his hand.*) Do as you like!
ANNA: Please, leave us now, Mr. Bugrov. Excuse us.... Please go.
BUGROV: Very good, ma'am. (*He gets up.*) So, don't worry. You can stay here till Christmas. I'll be dropping in tomorrow or the day after. Good-bye, ma'am. (*He goes out.*)
ANNA: We leave here tomorrow. Yes, now I've remembered—Platonov... So that's why he's running away!
VOYNITSEV: Let them do what they like. Let them take everything. I haven't a wife any more, so I don't want anything! I have no wife, Mother!
ANNA: No, you haven't. But what did he find in that scatter-brained little ninny Sophia? What did he find in that stupid girl? What could he have found in her? How undiscriminating these foolish men are! They're capable of falling in love with any tr... And where were you all the time, husband? Where were your eyes? Cry baby! Snivelling while his wife was being snatched away from under his very nose. And he calls himself a man! [Why, you're just a stupid boy. Such stupid boys as you are married off only to be made a laughing-stock of. The silly asses!] Neither of you is any good. Neither you, nor your Platonov. What a wretched business this is!
VOYNITSEV: Nothing can help me now, least of all your reproaches. She's no longer mine and he's no longer yours. There's nothing more to say. [Leave me, mother. You can't bear my stupid face, can you?]
ANNA: But what are we to do? Something must be done. We must save what can be saved.
VOYNITSEV: Save? The only one who has to be saved is me. They seem to be happy so far. (*He sighs.*)
ANNA: You and your logic! It's they who ought to be saved, not

you. Platonov does not love her! Do you realize that? He seduced her as you once seduced that stupid German girl of yours! He does not love her! I'm sure of that. What did she tell you? Why don't you speak?

VOYNITSEV: She said she was his mistress.

ANNA: She's his fool, not his mistress. Shut up! Perhaps things can still be put right. Platonov is quite capable of making a hell of a fuss if a woman just kisses him or presses his hand. I'm sure things haven't gone too far with them yet. I'm sure of that.

VOYNITSEV: They have!

ANNA: You don't understand anything.

Enter MARY GREKOV.

MARY (*entering*): So that's where you are! Good morning. (*She shakes hands with* Anna.) Good morning, Mr. Voynitsev. I'm sorry, I believe I've disturbed you. An uninvited guest is worse, worse ... how does it go?—oh, yes—worse than a Tartar. I've only looked in for a moment. You can't imagine what happened! (*She laughs.*) I must show it to you, Anna ... Excuse us, Mr. Voynitsev. I've something to tell your mother in confidence. (*She takes* Anna *aside.*) Read this. (*She gives her a note.*) I received it yesterday. Read it!

ANNA (*quickly reading the note*): Oh! ...

MARY: You know I summonsed him. (*She lays her head on* Anna's *bosom.*) Please send for him, Anna, please!

ANNA: What do you want him for?

MARY: I'd like to see what he looks like now. I'd like to see what's written on his face. Please, send for him! I beg you! I'd like to say a few words to him. You don't know what I've done. (*In a whisper.*) I've been to see the inspector of schools. Mr. Platonov will be transferred at my request. Oh, what have I done! (*She cries.*) Send for him! I couldn't have known that he'd write this letter, could I? Oh, if only I'd known it. Oh, I'm so sorry!

ANNA: Go into the library, my dear. I'll join you in a minute and we'll have a talk. I have to say a few words to Sergey.

MARY: The library? All right. But you will send for him, won't you? I'd like to see what he looks like after this letter. You've read it, haven't you? Give it back to me. I'll hide it. (*She hides the letter.*) Oh, my dear, my sweet Anna, I beg you! I'll go, but do send for him. [Don't listen, Mr. Voynitsev. Let's talk in German. *Schicken Sie, meine Liebe.*]

ANNA: All right. Please go now.

MARY: All right. (*She kisses her quickly.*) Don't be angry with me, my dear Anna. I'm suffering! You can't imagine what I feel. I'm going, Mr. Voynitsev. You can go on with your conversation. (*She goes out.*)

ANNA: I'll find out everything now. Don't get excited! Perhaps your marriage can still be patched up. What a terrible business! Who could have expected it? I'll go and have a talk with Sophia at once. I'll try and find out everything from her. You're mistaken and you're making a fool of yourself! Still, perhaps I'm wrong! (*She covers her face with her hands.*) No, no, it can't be!

VOYNITSEV: Yes, it can! I'm not mistaken!

ANNA: I'd still like to have a talk to her. I'll have a talk to him, too.

VOYNITSEV: Go and talk to them. It's a waste of time. (*He sits down at the table.*) [Let's go away from here. There's no hope. There isn't even a straw at which we could clutch.]

ANNA: I'll find out everything out at once. [You can stay here and cry. You'd better go to bed, you grown-up man!] Where's Sophia?

VOYNITSEV: In her room, I suppose.

ANNA *goes out.*

VOYNITSEV: What a catastrophe! How long will it drag on, I wonder. Tomorrow, the day after tomorrow, a week, a month, a year! There's no end to my torment! I ought to shoot myself.

PLATONOV (*enters with his arm in a sling*): [There he sits. He's weeping, I think. (*Pause.*) Peace be to your soul, my poor friend! (*He walks up to* Voynitsev.)] For God's sake, Sergey listen to me! I haven't come here to justify myself. [It's not for you or for me to judge me.] I have come to plead for you, not for myself. I'm pleading with you as a brother. Hate me, despise me, think what you like of me, but do not kill yourself! I'm not talking of revolvers. I mean, by slow stages. You are not strong. Grief will kill you. [I won't go on living. I'll kill myself. Don't you do it. Do you want me to die?] Do you want me to put an end to my life? (*Pause.*)

VOYNITSEV: I don't want anything.

ANNA (*coming in*): He's here? (*She walks up slowly to* Platonov.) Is it true, Platonov?

PLATONOV: It's true.

ANNA: He dares—he dares to speak so calmly. It is true then. You despicable man, you knew that it was despicable, didn't you?

PLATONOV: Despicable man . . . Can't you be a little more civil? I knew nothing. All I knew and still know is that I had no intention of inflicting a thousandth part of the torment he's feeling now!

ANNA: You should also have known that the wife of one friend should not become the plaything of another, shouldn't you? (*She shouts.*) You don't love her! You were just bored!

VOYNITSEV: Ask him why he has come, mother.

ANNA: It's despicable. It's despicable to play with the lives of people. They're the same flesh and blood as you are, you awfully clever man!

VOYNITSEV (*jumping up*): He has dared to come here! The impudence of the man! Why did you come here? I know why, but you won't impress or dazzle us with your high-sounding phrases.

PLATONOV: Who is 'us'?

VOYNITSEV: I know now the true value of all those high-sounding phrases of yours. Leave me alone! If you've come here to atone for your guilt by making fine speeches, then I'd like you to know that you won't succeed however brilliant your oratorical gifts.

PLATONOV: Just as one cannot atone for one's guilt by fine speeches, so one cannot prove anything by screams or by spite. I believe I told you that I intended to shoot myself.

VOYNITSEV: That's not the way one atones for one's guilt. Not by words, which I do not believe in now. I despise your words. That's how a Russian atones for his guilt. (*He points at something through the window.*)

PLATONOV: What's out there?

VOYNITSEV: There, by the wall, lies a man who has atoned for his guilt.

PLATONOV: Yes, I saw . . . But why are you indulging in high-sounding phrases? I believe you've just had a great shock. You've gone all to pieces now, and yet you're strutting about like some ham actor. What shall we ascribe this to: insincerity or stupidity?

VOYNITSEV (*sitting down*): Ask him why he's come here, Mother.

ANNA: What do you want here, Platonov?

PLATONOV: Why don't you ask me yourself? Why bother your mother? All's lost! [Your wife has left you and all's lost. Nothing is left. Beautiful as a day in May, Sophy's an ideal overshadowing all other ideals. A man without a woman is like a steam-engine without steam. The steam has evaporated and life's ruined. All's lost.] Honour, human dignity, noble lineage —everything! [The end has come.]

VOYNITSEV: I'm not listening. Please, leave me alone!

PLATONOV: Of course. Do not insult me, Sergey. I haven't come here to be insulted. Your misfortune does not give you the right to fling dirt at me. I'm a human being, so please treat me in a human way. You're unhappy, but your unhappiness is nothing compared with what I endured after you left me. Oh what a terrible night! Let me assure you, you—lovers of humanity,

that your unhappiness isn't worth a fraction of my own torments.
ANNA: Quite possibly. But who cares a rap for your torments or for what happened to you during the night.
PLATONOV: You don't care, either?
ANNA: Not a bit!
PLATONOV: Oh? Don't tell lies, Anna. (*He sighs.*) Well, perhaps you're right in your own way. Perhaps ... But where can I find human beings? Who can I turn to? (*He buries his face in his hands.*) Where are the human beings? They don't understand. They don't understand! Who will understand? They're stupid, cruel, heartless! ...
VOYNITSEV: Oh, I understand you. I understand you perfectly. It doesn't suit you at all, my dear sir, my ex-friend, to try to play on our feelings. I can see through you. A cunning scoundrel, that's what you are!
PLATONOV: I forgive you, fool that you are, for what you've just said. You'd better take care and say nothing more. (*To* Anna.) But what are you, a lover of violent emotions, hanging about here for? Curious? This is none of your business. We don't want any witnesses.
ANNA: This is none of your business, either. You can—clear out. The impudence of the man! To make mischief, play dirty tricks, behave like a cad, and then come here and complain about his torments! A diplomat! [However, I'm sorry. If you don't want to hear something more disagreeable,] you'd better go. [Do me a favour!]
VOYNITSEV (*jumping up*): What more does he want of me? What do you want? What do you expect me to do? I can't understand.
PLATONOV: I can see you don't understand. A grief-stricken man is right to go to a pub in search of solace. Yes, a thousand times right! (*He goes towards the door.*) I'm sorry I spoke to you, humiliated myself. I was stupid enough to take you for decent

people. You're just the same as anybody else—savages, coarse, uncouth peasants. (*Goes out slamming the door.*)

ANNA (*wringing her hands*): What an abominable thing to say! Go after him at once! Catch him up and tell him—tell him—

VOYNITSEV: What am I to tell him?

ANNA: [You'll know what to tell him . . .] Anything! Run, Sergey, I implore you. He meant well. You should have realized it, but you were so cruel to him. Run, darling.

VOYNITSEV: I can't! Leave me alone!

ANNA: But he's not the only one to blame! We're all to blame, Sergey. All of us have passions and none of us has the strength to resist them. Run! Be nice to him. Show him that you are a human being. For God's sake, go on, run!

VOYNITSEV: I'm going mad . . .

ANNA: Go mad! But don't dare to insult people. For goodness sake, run! (*She weeps.*) Please, Sergey!

VOYNITSEV: Leave me alone, Mother!

ANNA: Very well, I'll go myself. No, I can't . . . I—I can't run after him. I myself . . .

PLATONOV (*comes in*): Oh dear! (*He sits down on the sofa.*)

VOYNITSEV *gets up.*

ANNA (*aside*): What's the matter with him? (*Pause.*)

PLATONOV: My arm's aching. I'm as hungry as a starved dog. I'm cold. Feverish. I'm in pain. [Please, understand, I'm in pain! My life's finished. What do you want of me?] What more do you want of me? Isn't one night in hell enough for you?

VOYNITSEV (*walking up to* Platonov): Let's forgive and forget, Michael. I . . . You understand my position, don't you? Let's part friends. (*Pause.*) I forgive you. [On my word of honour, I do. If I could forget what's happened, I'd be as happy as I've never been before.] Let's leave each other in peace.

PLATONOV: Yes, let's. (*Pause.*) I'm afraid I've gone all to pieces. The machine is past repair. I feel terribly sleepy. I can hardly keep my eyes open and yet I can't sleep. I give in. I apologize. I plead guilty. I shan't say another word. Do what you like and think what you like. VOYNITSEV *goes away from* PLATONOV *and sits down at the table.* [I'm not leaving ... You can set the house on fire if you like. You can all leave the room if I disturb you.] (*He is about to lie down.*) Please, give me something warm ... Not to eat, but to cover myself with ... I'm not going home. It's raining. I'll lie down here.

ANNA (*walking up to* Platonov): Go home, Michael. I'll send along whatever you need or bring it myself. (*She touches him on the shoulder.*) Go on, go home.

PLATONOV: Anyone who objects to my being here can leave the room. Give me a drink of water. I want some water. (Anna *hands him a decanter of water.*) I'm ill. I'm very ill, my dear.

ANNA: Go home. (*She puts her hand on his forehead.*) His forehead's burning. Please, go home. I'll send for Triletsky.

PLATONOV (*softly*): I'm in a bad way, your ladyship. In a very bad way.

ANNA: What about me? Go, please. I beg you. You must go away! Do you hear?

SOPHIA *enters.*

SOPHIA: [Be so good as to take your money back. What generosity! I believe I told you already ... (*She sees* Platonov.)] You here? Why are you here? (*Pause.*) Funny ... What are you doing here?

PLATONOV: Me?

SOPHIA: Yes, you.

ANNA: We'd better leave, Sergey. (*She goes out, but after a minute tiptoes back and sits in a corner.*)

PLATONOV: It's all over, Sophia.

SOPHIA: You mean it?

PLATONOV: Yes, I mean it. [We'll talk later.

SOPHIA: What does it all mean, Michael?]

PLATONOV: I don't want anything. I don't want love, I don't want hatred. Just leave me alone, all of you! I beg you. I don't even feel like talking. I've had enough... Please...

SOPHIA: What is he saying?

PLATONOV: I'm saying that I've had enough. I don't want a new life. I don't know what to do with my old one. I don't want anything.

SOPHIA (*shrugging*): I don't understand!

PLATONOV: You don't understand? Our affair is at an end.

SOPHIA: You mean you're not going away with me?

PLATONOV: Don't take it to heart, Sophia... I mean, Mrs. Voynitsev.

SOPHIA: Behaving like a cad?

PLATONOV: I suppose so.

SOPHIA: You swine! (*She weeps.*)

PLATONOV: I know. I've heard it a hundred times before. [I only wish we could talk it over later and—without witnesses. (Sophia *bursts out sobbing.*) You'd better go to your room.] The most unnecessary thing in a crisis is tears. It had to happen and it did happen. Nature has its laws, and our life its logic. What happened is quite logical. (*Pause.*)

SOPHIA (*sobbing*): What has this to do with me? [What do I care whether you're tired or not? This has nothing to do with my life which you've taken away. What has this to do with me?] Don't you love me any more?

PLATONOV: Let this scandalous affair be a lesson to you in future. That's the only consolation I can offer you.

SOPHIA: How dare you say this to me! It's despicable!

PLATONOV: Why weep? Oh, I'm so sick of it all! (*Shouting.*) I'm ill!

SOPHIA: He swore he loved me. He begged. He started it all. And now... Don't you like me any more? You only needed me for two weeks? I hate you! I'm sick of the sight of you! Get out of here! (*She sobs more violently.*)

ANNA: Platonov!
PLATONOV: Well?
ANNA: Go away!

PLATONOV *gets up and goes slowly towards the door.*

SOPHIA: Wait! Don't go! Are you—in earnest? Are you sure you're not drunk? Please, sit down. Think it over. (*She seizes him by the shoulder.*)

PLATONOV: I've been sitting down and I've thought it over. I'm not your man, Sophia. I've been rotting away for such a long time that my soul has wasted away and there's no way of bringing me back to life. All you can do is to bury me as far away as possible so that I do not infect the air. Believe me, I beg you, for the last time.

SOPHIA (*wringing her hands*): But what am I going to do? What can I do? Tell me! I shall die. I shall never outlive this perfidy! I can't live for another instant! I'll kill myself! (*She sits down in an armchair in a corner of the room.*) What are you doing to me? (*She has hysterics.*)

VOYNITSEV (*going up to Sophia*): Sophy!

ANNA: My goodness, Sophy, do calm down! Give her some water, Sergey.

VOYNITSEV: Sophy, don't go on so! Stop it! Platonov, what are you waiting here for? Go, for God's sake!

ANNA: There, there Sophy, that'll do!

PLATONOV (*going up to* Sophia): What's all this about? Good Lord! (*He walks away quickly.*) The idiocy of it!

SOPHIA: Get away from me! All of you! I don't need your help. (*To* Anna.) Please, go away. I hate you! I know who I have to thank for all this. You'll pay for it!

ANNA: Hush, dear. We mustn't start quarrelling.

SOPHIA: Had it not been for your corrupting influence, he wouldn't have ruined me! (*She sobs.*) Go away! (*To* Voynitsev.) And you, too, go away from me.

VOYNITSEV *goes off to the table, sits down, and buries his head on his crossed arms.*

ANNA (*to* Platonov): Please go. You're quite extraordinarily idiotic today. What more do you want?

PLATONOV (*stopping up his ears*): Where can I go? I'm stiff with cold. (*He goes towards the door.*) Oh, I wish I was dead!

Enter TRILETSKY.

TRILETSKY [(*in the doorway*): I'll give you such an announcing your own mother won't know you.

YAKOV (*off stage*): It's master's orders.

TRILETSKY: Go and kiss your master. He's as big a fool as you are. (*He*] *comes in.*) So you're here, are you? (*He collapses on the sofa.*) This is terrible. This, this, this . . . (*He jumps up.*) Oh! (*To* Platonov.) The tragedy is almost at an end, tragedian! Yes, sir, almost at an end.

PLATONOV: What do you want?

TRILETSKY: [What are you wasting your time here for?] Where have you been gadding about, you poor wretch? Aren't you ashamed of yourself? Not feeling sorry, by any chance? Airing your views here, I suppose? Preaching your sermons?

PLATONOV: Talk sense, man! What do you want?

TRILETSKY: The sheer brutality of it! (*He sits down and covers his face with his hands.*) Oh, what a calamity!

[PLATONOV: What's happened?

TRILETSKY: What's happened? Don't you know? Don't you care? Are you too busy?

ANNA: What's the matter, Nicholas?]

PLATONOV: Is it Sasha? Speak, Nicholas! That's all we needed. What's happened to her?

TRILETSKY: She's poisoned herself with matches.

PLATONOV: What are you saying?

TRILETSKY (*shouts*): She's poisoned herself with matches! (*Jumping up.*) Here, read this! Read it! (*He thrusts a note under his eyes.*) Read it, philosopher!

PLATONOV (*reads*): 'It is sinful to pray for suicides, but pray for me, please. I have taken my life because I'm ill. Michael, love little Nicholas and my brother as I love you. Look after father. Live according to the law. Nicholas, my son, may the Lord bless you as I bless you with a mother's blessing. Forgive me, a sinful woman. The key to Michael's chest of drawers is in my woollen dress.' My treasure! Sinful? She sinful? That's all we needed! (*He clutches his head.*) Poisoned herself . . . (*Pause.*) Sasha's poisoned herself. Where is she? I'll go to her. (*Tears his sling off.*) I—I'll bring her back to life.

TRILETSKY (*lying down on the sofa face downwards*): Before talking of bringing her back to life you shouldn't have killed her first.

PLATONOV: Killed . . . Why do you say that, you crazy fool? I didn't kill her. Did I—did I want her to die? (*He weeps.*) Poisoned herself! That's all I needed! Crushed under a wheel like a dog! [If this is not punishment, then . . . (*He shakes his fist.*) It's a cruel, immoral punishment!] It's more than I can bear! [What for? Suppose I did sin, suppose I was a scoundrel —*I* am still alive! (*Pause.*) Look at me, all of you, look at me! A nice specimen, aren't I?

TRILETSKY (*jumping up*): Yes, yes, yes. Let's weep now. Particularly as we seem to have been doing so already. What you want is a good thrashing, my dear chap. Put your cap on and let's go, husband!] A fine husband you are! Ruined a woman for no reason at all. Brought her to a point where she committed suicide. And they are entertaining him here! They like him! An original fellow! An interesting man! The stamp of noble sorrow on his brow and traces of faded beauty! Come on, let's go. Have a look at what you've done, you interesting, original fellow!

PLATONOV: No more words, no more words! I don't want any words.

TRILETSKY: You're lucky I got there at daybreak this morning. [I don't know what would have happened if I hadn't looked in at home so early, if I hadn't been just in time!] She would have died! Do you understand that or not? You usually understand everything except the most ordinary things. [Oh, I'd have given you hell then! I wouldn't have taken any notice of your sorrowful countenance.] Had you wagged your damned tongue less and listened more this would never have happened! [I wouldn't exchange ten such clever fellows as you for her.] Come on!

VOYNITSEV: Don't shout, for God's sake. I'm sick of all of you.

TRILETSKY: Come on!

PLATONOV: Wait! So she—she's not dead, you say?

TRILETSKY: You'd rather she was, would you?

PLATONOV [(*shouting*)]: She's not dead! Can't make you out at all. She isn't dead, is she? (*He embraces* Triletsky.) She's alive! (*He bursts out laughing.*) Alive!

ANNA: I don't understand. Please explain, Triletsky. Everyone seems to be particularly stupid today. What's the meaning of this letter then?

TRILETSKY: She wrote this letter. If I hadn't been in time, she'd have been dead. She's still very ill. I don't know if her constitution will stand it. Oh, if she dies, I'll . . . (*To* Platonov.) Out of my sight!]

PLATONOV: You gave me such a fright. Thank God, she's still alive. [You didn't let her die, then. Oh, my dear. (*He kisses* Triletsky.) Oh, you dear fellow!] (*He laughs loudly.*) I never believed in medicine, but now I believe even in you! [How is she now? Weak, ill? We'll put her on her feet again.

TRILETSKY: Will she ever get over it, I wonder?

PLATONOV: She will! I'll see that she does. Why didn't you tell me at first that she was alive? Anna, my dear woman, a glass of cold water and I'm a happy man. Forgive me, all of you, all. Anna,

I'm going mad! (*He kisses* Anna's *hand.*) Sasha's alive. Water, water! (Anna *goes out with the empty decanter and comes back a minute later with it filled with water. To* Triletsky.) Come, let's go to her. We shall put her on her feet again. We'll turn the whole of medicine upside-down, from Hippocrates to Triletsky. Turn it all upside-down! Who but she should be alive?] All right, let's go. No, wait. My head's spinning. I'm terribly ill... Wait... (*He sits down on the sofa.*) Let me rest first, then we'll go. Is she very weak?

TRILETSKY: Yes, very. (*Pointing to* Platonov.) He's glad! I don't see what he's so glad about.

ANNA: I, too, was scared. You should have made everything clear at once. Drink! (*She offers the decanter to* Platonov.)

PLATONOV (*drinking avidly*): Thank you, kind woman. [I'm a scoundrel. Quite an extraordinary scoundrel! (*To* Triletsky.) Sit down beside me. (Triletsky *sits down.*) You're all in too. Thank you, my friend. Did she swallow much?

TRILETSKY: Enough to kill her.

PLATONOV: She of all people! Well, thank God. My arm's aching. More water, please.] I'm terribly ill myself, Nicholas. [Can scarcely hold my head up. May collapse any minute.] Must be running a temperature. Little soldiers in chintz uniforms and pointed caps keep flashing before my eyes. Everything's green and yellow. Let me have some quinine. Lots of it.

TRILETSKY: What you want is a good thrashing!

PLATONOV (*laughing at the top of his voice*): Always joking. You see, sometimes I do laugh at your jokes. Oh, I feel so ill. You can't imagine how ill I am! (Triletsky *feels his pulse.*)

ANNA (*softly to* Triletsky): Take him away, Nicholas. I'll come and see you later and have a talk with Sasha. [Fancy her giving us such a fright. She isn't in danger, is she?

TRILETSKY: Impossible to say anything yet. She didn't manage to poison herself, but I'm afraid she's in a bad way.

PLATONOV: What did you give her?

TRILETSKY: I gave her what was necessary. (*He gets up.*)] Come on, we're going.

[PLATONOV: And what did you give Anna just now?

TRILETSKY: You're imagining things. Come along!]

PLATONOV: Yes, let's go. (*He gets up.*) Sergey, forget it! (*He sits down.*) Forget it. What are you so cut up about? [Just as if the sun had been stolen from the earth.] A student of philosophy, too. Be a second Socrates. Eh, Sergey? (*Softly.*) I don't know myself what I'm talking about.

[TRILETSKY (*putting his hand on* Platonov's *head*): Don't you get ill. Though, I suppose, an illness wouldn't do you any harm now, just to clear your conscience.]

ANNA: Platonov, please go now. [Send to town for another doctor. A consultation might help. I'll send for one myself.] Don't worry. And please tell Sasha not to worry, either.

PLATONOV: There's a tiny baby piano crawling along on your bosom, Anna. What fun! (*He laughs.*) Great fun! Sit down, Nicholas. Play something on it. (*He laughs loudly.*) Great fun! I'm ill, Nicholas. Seriously ill. I'm not joking. Come on, let's go.

COL. TRILETSKY *enters, dishevelled, in a dressing gown.*

COL. TRILETSKY: My poor Sasha! (*He weeps.*)

TRILETSKY: That finishes it! You and your tears. Go away. What have you come running here for?

COL. TRILETSKY: She's dying. She's asking for a priest. [I'm afraid —oh, I'm so afraid.] (*He goes up to* Platonov.) Michael, I implore you, dear, clever, honest man, go and tell her that you love her. Forget all these disgusting love affairs of yours. I beg you on my bended knees. You see, she's dying! She's the only daughter I have. The only one. [If she dies, it'll be the end of me, too. I'll drop dead—there won't even be time to fetch a priest.] Tell her that you love her, that she's still your wife. Set her mind at rest, for God's sake. My dear fellow, one has to lie sometimes to save a life. Damn you, I know you're honest, but tell a lie for once to save the life of one who's so near and dear to you. [Come, let's go to her! Do me, an old man, this favour, for God's sake. The Lord will reward you a hundredfold. I'm shaking all over with fear.]

PLATONOV: Have you been drinking, Colonel? (*Laughs.*) We'll get Sasha well and then have a drink together. Lord, I'm so thirsty!

COL. TRILETSKY: Come, let's go, [most honourable and most righteous man.] Say a couple of words to her and she'll be saved. Medicine won't help, when her mind's suffering.

TRILETSKY: Will you please leave us for a minute, Father? (*He takes his father by the sleeve and leads him to the door.*) Who told you that she was going to die? What put that idea into your head? She isn't in danger at all. Wait in the next room, please. We'll go to her at once. You ought to be ashamed to burst in here like this.

COL. TRILETSKY (*to* Anna): You shouldn't have done it, Diana. God won't forgive you. [He's a young man, inexperienced.]

TRILETSKY (*pushing him into the next room*): Wait there! (*To* Platonov.) Are you coming?

PLATONOV: I'm terribly ill, Nicholas.

TRILETSKY: Are you coming or not, I ask you?

PLATONOV (*getting up*): Don't talk so much. My throat's parched. What can I do about it? All right, let's go. I wasn't wearing a hat when I came here, was I? (*He sits down.*) Look for my hat, please.

SOPHIA: He should have foreseen it. I gave myself to him without asking questions. I knew I was killing my husband, but I—I stopped at nothing for his sake. (*She gets up and goes up to* Platonov.) What have you done to me? (*She sobs.*)

TRILETSKY (*clutching his head*): Good Lord! (*He walks up and down the stage.*)

ANNA: Compose yourself, Sophy. This isn't the time. He is ill.

SOPHIA: How is it possible to play with a human life? Is it the sort of thing a humane person would do? (*She sits down beside* Platonov.) My whole life's ruined. I'm no longer alive now. Save me, Platonov! It isn't too late! Platonov, it is not too late! (*Pause.*)

ANNA (*weeping*): Sophy . . . what do you want? There'll be plenty of time for this later. What can he say to you now? Didn't you hear? Didn't you hear?

SOPHIA: Platonov . . . I ask you again . . . (*She sobs.*) No? (Platonov *moves away from her.*) You don't want me . . . All right then. (*She goes down on her knees.*) Platonov!

ANNA: This has gone too far, Sophy. Don't dare do that! No man deserves that a woman should go down on her kness before him. (*She lifts her up and makes her sit down.*) You—a woman!

SOPHIA (*sobbing*): Please, tell him . . . Persuade him . . .

ANNA: You must pull yourself together. You must be . . . strong. You are a woman! Come, go back to your room. (*Pause.*) Go and lie down. (*To* Triletsky.) What are we to do with her, Nicholas?

TRILETSKY: You'd better ask our dear, charming Michael about it. (*He walks up and down the stage.*)

ANNA: Let's put her to bed, Sergey. Nicholas, help me, will you?

VOYNITSEV *gets up and goes up to* SOPHIA.

TRILETSKY: Yes, let's take her to her room. I'd better give her a sedative.

ANNA: I feel like having a sedative myself. (*To* Voynitsev.) Be a man, Sergey. You, at least, must keep your head. I don't feel any better than you, but I'm still on my feet. Come along, Sophy. What a day! (*They lead* Sophia *off.*) Courage, Sergey! Let's behave like sensible people.

VOYNITSEV: I'll do my best, Mother. I'll do my best.

TRILETSKY: Don't worry too much, Sergey. We'll pull you through. You're not the first and you won't be the last.

VOYNITSEV: I'll do my best. Yes, I'll do my best.

They go out.

PLATONOV: A cigarette, Nicholas, and a drink of water. (*He looks round.*) Have they gone? I must go too. (*Pause.*) I have ruined weak women—women innocent of any offence. It wouldn't have been so bad if I'd killed them some other way, under the pressure of some monstrous passion, Spanish fashion. But somehow I've killed them so—stupidly, Russian fashion. (*He waves his hand in front of his eyes.*) Spots before my eyes. Little clouds. I suppose I shall be raving soon. I feel crushed, flattened, pulverized. It was not so long ago that I stopped strutting about, was it? (*He buries his face in his hands.*) Oh, God, I'm so ashamed! I ache with shame! I was hungry, cold, worn out, my whole life was a fake, I came to this house . . . and . . . they offered me a warm corner, they clothed me, they showered their affection on me as on no one else—and that's how I've repaid them! But then, I'm ill. Bad . . . Must kill myself . . . (*He goes up to the table.*) A regular arsenal! Choose any weapon you like. (*He picks up a revolver.*) Hamlet was afraid of dreams. I'm afraid of —life. What's going to happen to me if I go on living? I shall be ashamed to face people. (*He puts revolver to his temple.*) *Finita la commedia.* One clever scoundrel less in the world! Forgive me my sins, O Lord! (*Pause.*) Well? So, it's death Now? You can go on aching, arm, as much as you like now. (*Pause.*) No, I haven't the strength. (*He puts the revolver down on the table.*) I want to live. (*He sits down on the sofa.*) I want to live. (Mary *enters.*) Water . . . Where's Nicholas? (*Seeing* Mary.) Who's this? Ah! (*He laughs.*) My mortal enemy! Shall we go to court tomorrow? (*Pause.*)

MARY: After the letter you've written me, we're no longer enemies.

PLATONOV: Makes no difference. No more water?

MARY: Do you want a drink of water? What's the matter with you?

PLATONOV: I'm ill. I'm probably getting a fever. [I liked that letter. Very clever. But it would be cleverer still if you didn't have anything to do with me] . . . wanted to shoot myself . . .

(*He laughs.*) Couldn't do it. Instinct of self-preservation . . . Your brain tells you one thing, nature another. Sharp-eyed aren't you? You're a clever girl. (*He kisses her hand.*) Your hand's cold. Will you do something for me?

MARY: Yes, yes, yes. . . .

PLATONOV: Take me home with you. I'm ill. My throat's parched. I'm suffering terribly, unbearably! I want to sleep, but there's nowhere to lie down. I'd be glad if you could find some place for me. A barn, or something. A place to lie down in . . . some water and a little . . . quinine. Please! (*He holds out his hand to her.*)

MARY: Yes, let's go! I'll be delighted. You can stay at my house as long as you please. [I'm afraid you don't know what I've done. Come, let's go!]

PLATONOV: Many thanks, clever little girl. A cigarette, water, and a bed. [Is it raining?

MARY: Yes.

PLATONOV: We'll have to drive in the rain.] We shan't be taking each other to court, shall we? Peace! (*He looks at her.*) I'm not raving, am I?

MARY: Not at all. Let's go. My carriage is covered.

PLATONOV: You're a pretty thing . . . Why are you blushing? I shan't touch you. Just kiss your cold little hand. (*He kisses her hand and draws her to himself.*)

MARY (*sitting on his lap*): No, I mustn't! (*She gets up.*) Let's go. Why do you look at me like that? Let go of my hand!

PLATONOV: Sorry, I'm ill. (*He gets up.*) Let's go. Let me kiss your cheek. (*He kisses her cheek.*) No ulterior motive! [I can't . . . It's all a lot of nonsense, though.] Let's go, Mary, and as quickly as possible, please. Here . . . here's the revolver I wanted to shoot myself with. On the cheek . . . (*He kisses her on the cheek.*) I'm raving, but I can still see your face . . . I love all people! All! I love you, too. People have been dearer than anything to me.

I've never wanted to offend anyone and I've offended everyone
... everyone ... (*He kisses her hand.*)

MARY: I see it all. I understand your position. It's Sophy, isn't it?

PLATONOV: Sophy, Zizi, Mimi, there are lots of you. I love you all. When I was at the university I tried to help the women of the streets in Theatre Square. Used to say nice things to them. Everybody was in the theatre, but I was in the square. I bought Raissa out. Collected three hundred roubles from the students and bought another girl out, too. Shall I show you her letters?

MARY: What's the matter with you?

PLATONOV: You think I've gone mad? No. It's only my fever. I'm delirious. Ask Triletsky. (*He takes her by the shoulders.*) They love me, too, all of them. Even if I insult them, they love me. There was a girl—Mary her name was—I insulted her and pushed her onto a table. She, too, loves me. But you're Mary, aren't you? I'm sorry.

MARY: What's wrong with you?

PLATONOV: Platonov is wrong with me. You love me, don't you. You do? Tell me frankly. I don't want anything. Just tell me whether you love me or not.

MARY (*puts her head on his chest*): I do. Oh, I do.

PLATONOV (*kisses her head*): They all love me. When I get well I'll make a strumpet of you. Before, I used to say nice things to them, but now I'm making strumpets of them all.

MARY: I don't care. I don't want anything. You're the only man I want. I don't want to know anyone else. Do anything you like with me. You—you're the only man I want. (*She cries.*)

PLATONOV: Now I understand why Oedipus tore out his eyes! How base I am, and how deeply conscious I am of my own baseness! Go away! It's not worth it. I'm ill. (*He frees himself.*) I shall be going now. I'm sorry, Mary. I'm going mad! Where's Triletsky?

SOPHIA *enters, goes up to the table and rummages about on it.*

MARY (*seizes* Platonov's *hand*): Shhhh. (*Pause.*)

SOPHIA *picks up the revolver, fires at* PLATONOV *and misses.*

MARY (*placing herself between* Platonov *and* Sophia): What are you doing? (*Shouts.*) Help! Here! Quick!
SOPHIA: Out of my way! (*She runs round* Mary *and shoots* Platonov *point-blank in the chest.*)
PLATONOV: Wait, wait . . . What's all this? (*He falls.*)

ANNA, COL. TRILETSKY, TRILETSKY, *and* VOYNITSEV
rush into the room.

ANNA (*wrenching the revolver from* Sophia's *hand, throws it down on the sofa*): Platonov! (*She bends over* Platonov.)

VOYNITSEV *covers his face and turns away to the door.*

TRILETSKY (*bends over* Platonov *and hastily unbuttons his coat*). (*Pause.*) Michael, can you hear me? (*Pause.*)
ANNA: For God's sake, Platonov! Michael, Michael. Do something, Nicholas!
TRILETSKY (*shouting*): Water!
MARY (*handing him the decanter*): Save him! You will save him, won't you? (*She walks agitatedly up and down the stage.*)

TRILETSKY *drinks the water and pushes the decanter aside.*

COL. TRILETSKY (*clutching his head*): Didn't say I was done for? Well, I am! (*He kneels.*) Lord Almighty, I'm done for! I'm done for!

YAKOV, VASILY, KATYA, *and the* COOK *come in.*

MARKO (*entering*): From the Justice of the Peace. (*Pause.*)
ANNA: Platonov!

PLATONOV *half rising, looks at all the people in the room in turn.*

ANNA: Platonov! It's all right! Have a drink of water.

PLATONOV (*pointing to* Marko): Give him three roubles. (*He falls back and dies.*)

ANNA: Courage, Sergey! [It will all pass, Nicholas. It'll all pass ... Courage!

KATYA (*bowing down low before* Anna): I'm the one to blame, ma'am. It was me who delivered the note. It was the money that tempted me. I'm sorry, ma'am.

ANNA: Courage!] Don't let's lose our heads. He's only fainted. He'll be all right.

TRILETSKY (*shouting*): He's dead!

ANNA: No, no!

MARY *sits down at the table, looks at the note and cries bitterly.*

COL. TRILETSKY: God rest his soul ... Perished ... Perished ...

TRILETSKY: Life isn't worth more than a copeck! Good-bye, Michael! You've lost your copeck. What are you staring at? He shot himself. The party's over. (*He weeps.*) Who am I going to drink with at your wake now? Oh, the fools! They couldn't save Platonov. (*He gets up.*) Father, go and tell Sasha she can die now. (*Swaying, he goes up to* Voynitsev.) And what about you, Sergey? Oh! (*He embraces* Voynitsev.) Platonov is dead. Our Platonov is dead. (*He sobs.*)

VOYNITSEV: What are we going to do now, Nicholas?

TRILETSKY: Bury the dead and mend the living.

ANNA (*rising slowly and going up to* Sophia): Compose yourself, Sophy. (*She sobs.*) Oh, what have you done? But ... but compose yourself. (*To* Triletsky.) Don't say anything to Sasha, Nicholas. I'll tell her myself. (*She goes up to* Platonov *and kneels.*) Platonov! My life! I can't believe it! You're not dead, are you? (*She takes his hand.*) My life!

TRILETSKY: We've got work to do, Sergey! We must help your wife and then ...

VOYNITSEV: Yes, yes ...

COL. TRILETSKY: The Lord has forsaken us For our sins. For my sins. Why did you sin, you old clown? Killed God's own creatures, drank, swore, condemned people. . . . The Lord couldn't put up with it any more and struck you down.

END OF ACT FOUR